The Urban

Dilys Gater

www.capallbann.co.uk

The Urban Shaman

©Copyright Dilys Gater 2005

ISBN 186163 227 4

Cover design by Paul Mason

Published by:

Capall Bann Publishing
Auton Farm
Milverton
Somerset
TA4 1NE

The urban shaman is like a flower that grows from a crack in the concrete

David Lawson
So You Want to Be a Shaman

The shaman knows his place
He is not a magus or master but a servant
He is the servant of the universe, of nature,
On all levels, in all worlds
He does not make decisions or choices
He has learned the wisdom to be silent
He does only what is necessary
To maintain the balance.

To my husband Paul

Yn yr enw
Apollo Belenos, goleu a than
Heb ddiwedd, yn dy garu du

All of the pictures in this book (apart from pages 10, 55, 67, 101, 103, 167, 195 and 198) are by Mark Campbell

Contents

Introduction

Who or what is a shaman? The more one seeks to find an answer to this question, the more the question itself becomes impossible to answer. The shaman is not a person but a shifting presence behind a mask that changes even as you think you have pinned it down.

No true shaman will ever make any claim to be 'qualified' – or indeed, to be anything. It is impossible to follow courses of study which equip you for the shamanic role, for the essence of the shaman is that he or she has learned to transcend mere existence. He or she will say only 'I am what I am – and the "I" that I am is unimportant'. I once wrote the following lines, feeling them to be the truest expression of which I was capable of explaining 'what' my psychic books are about and the work I do: they are a prayer in submission and celebration to the sources of my being as well as, hopefully, a message to any who might feel impelled to consult me.

The power I have is what you give to me
What I can accomplish is what you believe I can do
Your want and your need creates me.

Much mention is made of the shamanic journey by which enlightenment is achieved. But the shamanic journey encompasses and reflects the whole journey through this life and beyond. It is not an achieving but an awakening. When the first painful process of initiation has been passed – and at every stage further on - the initiate is only made more aware than ever of his or her own personal inadequacy and need for further progress.

phy.
may be
experience.

winners of the Nobel prize – who may in shamanic terms be
mere posturing children. The assumption that having been
alive for a long time bestows an automatic qualification for
anything is actually rather ridiculous.

In the work I do I have found that assumptions are generally
there to be challenged. The assumption for instance that
because the shaman's role brings him or her into close
awareness of the natural world – among other things –
aspirants must 'go back to nature', escape the toils and
traumas of civilisation and take themselves apart. Seek quiet
places where animals and plants are free in their natural
abundance in order to communicate with them. Remove
themselves from contamination by the unenlightened masses
who choke the streets of towns and cities and recognise only
'like minds', shun the pollution of noise, light, dirt – indeed,
almost all the components of ordinary living. Boring medio-
crity, the everyday grind and all the pinpricking problems of
struggling and squalling humanity – these, it is commonly
felt, have little to do with elevated mystical vision and the
work of the shaman.

This ideal has to be, even if only so that we can aspire to it.
But I personally found that although I tried (sometimes very
strenuously) to remove myself from all material hustle and
hubbub into circumstances and states of mind more conducive
to peace and the inspirational communion with other less
stressful – or indeed, distressful - worlds it was not to be. This
was not what the fates planned for me. Instead they had me
living and working in London for ten years, my spiritual and
psychic development progressing against the backdrop of the

8

Flicking through a book recently, I came across this line: *The urban shaman is like a flower that grows from a crack in the concrete.'* And to me, that spoke volumes. It seemed to validate much that I had previously found difficult to justify or even comprehend myself about my own experience.

For I actually loved living in London. Unlike most city dwellers, I had no desire to escape to some rose-covered cottage in the country or even a villa in Spain in order to be able to achieve peace with myself. Yes, I found London loud, fast, sometimes terrifying, always trailing her dirty skirts as it were, beneath the glitter and the glamour. But I was glad to be there and a part of it all, proud to belong, to be a Londoner. In fact, though I had been born and brought up in Wales I had never realised how deep my ancestral roots on my father's side went. Dad (who never quite lost his Cockney accent) was a Londoner, his family from generations of true East Enders.

We do not all need the wide open spaces of the country to find the spiritual awareness of the shaman within ourselves; it is not even necessary to long to 'get away' from the city. You carry the sacred space and the doorways into the Otherworlds within your own head.

Over the years I have tried to make sitters and patients aware of that space and those doorways in the most unlikely of settings – carrying out healing in a gym, for instance, where we are not able to shut out the beat of pop music from the on-going aerobics class next door. Or holding the hands of a sitter and patient amid the clatter of a McDonalds or afternoon tea at Harrods while talking to them about suffering and loss and bereavement and the dark night of the soul. I looked into the eyes of Cerberus, the great hound who guards the entrance to the Underworld, at midnight on the Victoria Line approaching Finsbury Park Tube station; and I have talked to denizens of that world sitting on the steps at Waterloo.

This book is — and has to be — a personal interpretation of what the role of an urban shaman involves. To me it is about the rightness of just being there, even if 'there' is one of the most frenetic of cities; about learning to be aware that sooty London pigeons, police horses and poodles in 'Pooch's Parlours' are just as relevant and as valuable as white owls and golden eagles. About knowing you can meet angels at Marble Arch or find, in the words of the poet, that Jacob's ladder stretches between 'Heaven and Charing Cross'.

This is a workbook in the sense that each chapter explores a different aspect of the shaman's role and is filled like the 'medicine bundle' of native shamans or the 'crane-bag' of Celtic tradition with a variety of objects - personal experience, thought and comment of my own as well as more general follows each chapter to help the aspirant with daily discipline: each contains thoughts for reading and meditation taken from my own spiritual teachers. Three main sources of instruction emerged for me which, though personal to my own needs, are nevertheless universal in their wisdom and cannot be regarded solely as 'mine'. There are practical work suggestions for the reader to follow to understand and begin to develop his or her shamanic abilities and potential.

Unless otherwise stated, the short verses and passages of prose used throughout the text to underline the themes treated and provide a basis for reflection originally appeared in *Astral Sex: A Journey*, written by myself and my husband Paul Gater. My contributions are marked with my initials, Paul's are marked PG and reproduced with his permission.

Lastly, though spiritual and psychic development makes no distinction between male and female and this book is for everyone, I have for the sake of convenience referred to the novice – and the shaman – throughout as 'he'.

Chapter 1

An Undiscovered Country -
from whose bourn no traveller returns

Uncharted territory, the road winding
dim in the half-light, glowing palely,
leading between hills of darkness –
to what inn where faery magic cannot work?
to what sea of boundless imagining?
to what other undiscovered countries
past imagining, silver with trumpets?
There have been other journeys,
neon-lit, rawly exposed, shrill,
with the choreographed deliberation of some ancient ballet
or impromptu, strawberries in dry summer.

But not this ritual of stillness, awe and wonder.
Time no longer, only is.
Centuries of tending the altar flame
For at last, the sight of the god.

DG

The London years. My first ten years of conscious spiritual growth, living and working as a psychic. They were intensely lived and magical years that provided a forty-something woman who feared the best part of her life was behind her with the most thrilling adventure she had ever undertaken or tradition, deep into the heart of the concrete jungle to find lost tribes and learn the secrets of ancient wisdom.

For most of that time I have to admit I felt little affinity with what I understood to be the shamanic way of life. I actually knew next to nothing about what it entailed but was never tempted to pursue the matter, since what I did encounter only had the effect of putting me off even further. It all seemed so vague, so nebulous. There did not appear to be any definitions or boundaries. Did 'New Age' hippyism or a habit of psychedelic drug-taking make one a shaman? What did you have to believe in to follow this way of life? And exactly what way of life was involved anyway?

I heard about courses on various aspects of shamanism that were offered in 'Mind, Body, Spirit' connections and even took part in some of the sessions myself – dancing to drumming, invoking my totem animal and visiting natural sites to welcome the seasons and the sun and moon. I became familiar with the names of authority figures, titles of classic books on subjects that included the role and work of the shaman; I spoke to individuals who had lived with the Native American Indians on their reservations or spent time with other followers of shamanically orientated belief systems, studying their traditions.

I was not, on the whole, impressed. It appeared that the aspiring shaman was required to be widely travelled, particularly experienced in physically difficult terrain and familiar with places like South America or Tibet. Some of the individuals I encountered claimed personal instruction by the medicine man or wise elder of tribes in these far-flung environments, even that they had been subjected to mysterious, often painful initiation ceremonies with the result that they were now shamans themselves. I found many of those self professed leaders of the people arrogant and self-opinionated, but on the other hand I felt no better disposed towards those at the other extreme who, with often painful simplicity, explained their ideas of removing themselves entirely from civilisation as we know it in dogged attempts to live their lives shamanically. The aim seemed to involve giving up all modern facilities and reverting entirely to a primitive existence of basic subsistence along the lines of dwellers in Third World countries. Such ideas struck me as idealistic and unworkable, eccentric or just plain pointless.

Shamanism appeared (in my view) to deify the masochistic. Wanting to make life especially hard by point-blank refusal of any and all assistance that would ease the burden seemed to invalidate what I personally had found to be the most unexpectedly joyous blessings of spiritual enlightenment - plain common sense and a sense of humour. What was wrong with making the most of a few creature comforts, particularly when like me, one was growing older? I had spent a country childhood growing up in the post-war years in a home where money was extremely tight and was very appreciative of, and thankful for the little luxuries (constant hot water! central heating!) of my tiny one-room flat in London.

And what was wrong with living in the city? I personally had no illusions about the romantic benefits of a 'primitive' and back-to-nature lifestyle. The hills and valleys of North Wales where I was born and their magical legacy had been bred in my bones – to the extent that I had written as my third psychic book one which reflected this called *Celtic Wise Woman* - but I had matured enough to realise one did not have to be sentimental about living a life of back-breaking labour in some sort of damp, unhygienic hovel miles from civilisation, even if it did have a view. By the time I started to work as a psychic I had developed enough self-esteem, I hoped, to allow myself the luxury of honesty, able to admit for instance that I personally much preferred the exercise

14

Norfolk, where my daughter now lived. . . or years I had made no secret of the fact that I found the warm cosy fug of a coffee- or tea-shop where I could sit comfortably reading, or getting to grips with my notes and my writing, far more of a spiritual home than any Andean mountain-top or wind-swept Hebridean beach. Did this automatically rule out the possibility of any shred of spiritual awareness or sensibility within my soul?

Expeditions Into the Interior

My main objection to shamanism as I encountered it was that there seemed to be very much of a double standard involved here. A lot of claims and generalisations were made but I could discover nothing definite about the role, work or lifestyle of anyone I identified as a 'real' shaman, a truly wise person whose authority I could respect. Try though I might, I grew frustrated because it seemed I could not find anyone of this calibre.

Instead I got to know and recognise the 'weekend shamans', people who had a day job of the nine-to-five variety which gave them a very comfortable existence they seemed happy to accept as necessary and appropriate, but who assured me with loud insistence that their real dream was to be able to give it up, since none of it mattered to them at all. They made a great show of turning their backs on civilisation (leaving Range Rovers and BMWs behind) in their 'quality' time. In designer casuals and footgear they headed for the great outdoors, preferring mountains, moors or islands I gathered, particularly if uninhabited by the white man (difficult to find in the UK). Consequently they were likely to be either coming or going from places like the coral reefs, jungles and rainforests of the South Seas, South America or India where the truly enlightened could be genuinely free spirits and communicate with nature in the rawest.

As a psychic employed on circuits that covered the whole of Southern England, I was learning all the time through practical experience as well as theoretical study. I encountered and worked with every kind of psychic, seer, diviner, healer, medium and practitioner of arcane magick. Many of them were extremely colourful and sometimes more difficult than prima donnas – but it was the wannabe shamans that I inevitably found most avoidable whenever our paths crossed. Let me tell you about some of them.

Individuals or groups of enthusiasts who ostentatiously wore totem claws or feathers round their necks, tramping miles beneath the great arch of the sky interacting with trees and waters and making it clear they were intensely physically aware. They were usually difficult to satisfy regarding refreshments since they were vegetarians or even vegans (at least for the duration). They avoided tea and coffee as though it was poison, preferring barleycorn or water drinks (oh! including of course, plenty of 'real ale'). They insisted on spending nights beneath the stars if possible, and if one had to share accommodation they preferred as rudimentary a tent or dormitory as they could get away with, renouncing the facilities of modern living in order to participate in a sense of 'true community'. (I soon learned that this might mean communal washing, bathing and every other kind of personal interaction). They insisted that everyone else sat with them round the camp-fire, performed rain-dances, learned how to 'be a tree' in Tai Chi classes and loved everybody else (often with embarrassing intensity) so long as they were 'like minded' and happened to be doing the same.

I came to know that 'job descriptions' are irrelevant in spiritual and psychic work and that even from the point of view of the enquirer, labels are not necessary. The seeker will always be drawn to the person he or she needs to consult and what is needed at any given time will always be found. But in spite of whatever claims were made or not made, and after ever met a true ... shamanism. Suspecting that it was my own innate snobbery and condescension (faults I was quite willing to admit to) that was behind my attitude I was reluctant to share my opinions with others even though I saw no reason to change them; and it was a long time before I was able to appreciate my own true faults and the real reasons why all my efforts to meet a 'real' shaman had met a blank.

For my own true lack was of genuine humility, genuine understanding that the way of the seeking soul can take many forms, and that each of them is equally real, equally truthful, however superficial it might seem to the arrogant and judgmental superiority of others. I also learned that it is not necessary to be able to approve of or even like what one's fellows are or do in order to follow one's own spiritual path. In earnestly striving forward oneself, one recognises the common goal of all, and the barriers of approval or disapproval simply remove themselves, dissolving like morning mist in the strengthening light of the sun.

But you might wonder how, particularly in a place like London, so far removed from indigenous tribes and their sacred sites, particularly blinded by my own judgmental and superior attitude, I came to meet and know my own Wise One, the teacher who would instruct me personally. Where and how did I come to hear the informed, authoritative voice that was to guide my faltering steps as a novice?

We can never recognise our ignorance while we are prisoners of it. Everything I thought I knew about the shaman's role and the shamanic way of life proved false – even the fact that one has to actively attempt such a role or way of living at all.

For we do not choose what we are to be. We are what we are, and can only strive to become more fully the embodiment of what is continually being revealed to us, whether by our Spirit Guide, Higher Self or something else. We do not need to travel into uncharted territory, communicate with strange, lost tribes and be instructed by plumed elders in order to find the voice of wisdom. It speaks within each of us. It is our own voice and yet not our own, and the wisdom it reveals is what we always knew yet did not know that we knew. It is the still, small voice that will counsel and advise us when all the ranting and raving, the thundering, the passions and the furies have passed, if we will let it.

A shaman is a developing entity and that development never ends. He does not listen to some teacher or authority figure and 'learn' what is said so that, as an authority figure himself, he can then teach it to others. He remains constantly in touch with the source, constantly aware of his need for wisdom, constantly trying to keep the balance within and without himself.

There are many books which will provide information about shamans, the basic details any interested enquirer can easily discover.

*   That though no-one can tell you exactly where the term 'shaman' originated it is most commonly believed to have come from the word 'Saman' in the language of the Tungus peoples of Siberia and to mean 'one who knows'. Sometimes this definition is taken further to mean 'one who knows ecstatically'.

*   That a shaman is a person able to enter realities beyond normal awareness with the aim not only of becoming empowered but of helping both himself and others.

* That he traditionally enters other realms through spiritual excitement and states of trance, often induced by repetitive dancing or drumming; that he is able to separate his spirit from his body and journey into those realms – most usually some kind of Upper World and Lower World - returning safely when his mission is done.

* That he can communicate with the natural world and form protective relationships with beings who guide and guard him on his travels through time and space, often animals but sometimes other forms of spirit entities.

* That he has learned to conquer death by symbolically dying, allowing himself to be torn apart by forces outside himself and being reborn in truth and wisdom, thus becoming a source of knowledge, wisdom and truth himself.

These as well as other aspects of the shaman's role are explored in this book. But as we have seen, no amount of information actually brings us any closer to him. The language of the shaman has no words and the harder one tries to pin him down, the more elusive he becomes. He is not one person but many, each role he plays only one more aspect of the whole. Like a jewel, he is many faceted and as we will see, like a jewel reflects the light that passes through him, while possessing no light of his own.

Meeting the Unknown

I did not become aware of my own psychic potential until I was in my mid-forties, by which time of course I had already chalked up quite a substantial amount of living and achieving. I was a writer and novelist, author of some sixty plus books. I had lived in North Wales, Chester and the Midlands, been married three times, had a grown-up daughter. But then, unexpectedly and inexplicably, my life took a dramatic new direction. I found myself on the brink of an entirely new beginning, my early years and achievements falling into place as no more than a kind of basic preparation, preliminary training as it were for what was to reveal itself as my true vocation, my real purpose in life.

In my tiny flat in London I was living alone for the first time, something I found frightening and challenging after suffering for years with emotional problems and being very dependent on the support of others. Mentally I was more vulnerable than I had ever been - physically not too brilliant either, since during my years as a psychic in London (I can see now that this was for a reason) I had a lot of health problems. Severe back trouble was the most limiting in that I was literally crippled as well as being in constant pain, though other more personal physical ailments of the type one is reluctant to admit to publicly, made my life even more uncomfortable and difficult. I was pushed to my physical limits and beyond them while also trying to educate myself in the disciplines and challenges of what I now felt to be my destined spiritual course.

The lifestyle I was now following was entirely different from any life I had previously known. It involved travelling several times a week and most weekends for long distances to attend Psychic Fairs and events in dozens of different venues that ranged from elegant ballrooms, Town Halls, five star hotels, the barns of country hostelries to Community, Health or Healing Centres (in one case, directly overlooking a busy learned the rules – that a psychic, like the actor I had always longed to be if I had not been a writer, was always in the spotlight, always on duty; that it was important to be there, not to let the public down; that however ill one felt one never missed a 'performance' but somehow struggled to make it, to be ready in costume and make-up for when the doors opened, when the 'curtain rose'.

I travelled to give consultations in private houses (from council semis to unbelievable mansions, one belonging to a Bollywood star) and saw sitters at home. I worked both as a psychic and a trader in Portobello Road and many of the other London markets. I carried out readings and gave healing in the most incongruous of settings that ranged from a converted railway carriage in Camden Market to 'car boots' in windy meadows, pouring rain or sub-zero temperatures; from 'stately homes', to marquees and tents, wine bars and coffee-shops, fashion and jewellery emporiums to a casino. I gave demonstrations and interviews in radio and TV studios and on location, from a candle-lit church to midnight 'phone-ins' sitting in my room in cosy dressing gown and slippers. Thank goodness there wasn't a video link! One of my associates went one better and could actually boast of being carried off by pirates - the pirate ship of Radio Caroline, in rough weather in the North Sea.

But though it was a stimulating, exciting life and I was learning all the time, I was extremely conscious of my need for instruction and tried several times at the beginning of my psychic development to find some group, class or circle I could join as a novice. As I have written elsewhere, though, the spirits to whom I now looked for guidance seemed to be making it very clear that I was going to have to work – and presumably also study - on my own. So with no real idea of what realms I might be entering – nor at that time, any real discriminatory experience of the different disciplines and sources of spiritual wisdom. I took the simplest, most obvious course, presenting myself humbly to the spirits. I prayed for help and guidance and then opened up my heart and mind to wait for whatever teaching I might be granted, whenever and however it might come.

None of the different cultural and belief systems – fascinating though they were - seemed the right one for me so I followed my own programme of prayer and discipline, setting aside time every day for meditation and communication with Spirit. I was ready to work regularly – every day if that proved feasible – with whatever teacher emerged to guide me, and had the vague aim of compiling some kind of personal handbook or reference work that I would be able to study both then and in the future.

After some time I began to be aware that I was receiving 'channelled' messages which I wrote down either in longhand or on my word processor. The material came from various sources: I identified one as 'the Goddess' and another was a very ancient civilisation I could not name. They were all enlightening and inspiring in their different ways, but again I did not feel they held the primary authority and consistency I was looking for. We are all given the instruction that is personal to us and will recognise the voice of our own teacher, our own guide when we encounter it – though as in my case, we may have no idea where it is to be found. As the often-repeated saying goes: 'When the pupil is ready, the teacher will appear'.

One evening when I sat down to work, I made a conscious prayer for more personal guidance, as a result of being told by somebody that one has to ask in order to meet up with one's Spirit Guide. (This is not actually always the case; though you can ask as much as you like, you will only be granted the awareness when and if you are ready to receive it). But my end of this chapter. They materialised over three consecutive days and I realised I had found the voice of my guide, adviser and source of wisdom; I had been honoured by awareness of the presence I would come to know as 'Mist'.

The voice of Mist, my principal spiritual guide and teacher, has always remained constant and Mist's guidance, advice, instruction and help has never failed me, though formal 'dialogues', conversations, question and answer sessions have continued only spasmodically over the years, as and when they were necessary. If I felt in particular need of enlightenment or encouragement, I would make contact and might spend several days or even weeks on a high spiritual level, writing down a great deal until I had worked through that particular problem or stage in my development. Then communication might lapse until a further time when, having reached a point where I was ready for more instruction, I was prompted to contact Mist again. The result has been that my own growth process is reflected in the material I have kept stored, proceeding in 'lesson periods' some of which were spaced months apart, while others followed closely on each other.

The relationship changed very significantly over the years. I became aware of Mist at first as an actual person, seeing 'him' for some time as I have described elsewhere as 'a silver man with no face'. I perceived 'his' presence as male and as in most similar partnerships between psychic or medium and his/her 'Spirit Guide' the relationship soon became the most significant and meaningful one in my life, deepening into such a close intimacy that communication could only be expressed at times in the most passionate endearments and the language of attachment and love. Such references are difficult to remove from the text and some have been left in this book where they occur.

Later I was able to perceive Mist not as a person but as an elevated being of no sex or form at all – a representation of some extremely advanced essence I am, in my human state, only able to appreciate as a fraction of its true force, wisdom and power I envisaged 'him' as the swirling silver mist of pure energy from which 'his' name was originally derived, though on one occasion when I was working on a sustained spiritual level, I 'saw' the form of Mist take on other images, one that looked like a bacteria or DNA sample seen through a microscope, a glimpse of life energy that perhaps strangely, made a great deal of sense to me. I have never worried about exactly 'who' or 'what' 'he' is. As I progressed, I discovered that my guide would appear whenever and in whatever form 'he' was needed, always providing what was necessary at that time whether I was aware enough to ask for what was needed or not.

Every individual will have his or her own unique experience in respect of 'Spirit Guides' or spirit connections and there is no one that is 'right'. But the experiences of others can perhaps help in the process of enlightenment. In my own case other, more recognisable 'Guides' made their appearance at various times as I progressed, providing their own uniquely valuable kinds of help and enlightenment, but Mist has remained my constant link with the Source. The early conversations I held with Mist are significant in a general sense as well as a personal one, for as with all spiritual teachings they reflect essential truths. Though we must all search for our own teacher, we will find in the end that the same teachings, the same truths are inherent everywhere, for there is only one source of truth. What is different, personal to each, is the way in which it is presented, in the best way for us, as individuals, to be able to read and learn.

I have included my early conversations with Mist in the following section as a general starting point for those in the position of the novice I was at the time they occurred. I was guide has given me over the years, may seem extremely simple but can be read on many levels. They are messages of great wisdom that, though often brief, prove on examination and consideration to contain volumes. Even now that I can appreciate more of their depth and complexity, I am sure I am still only scratching the surface.

Reference to the accounts of guidance received in traditional shamanic cultures will reveal that sometimes the teachers or advisers are perceived as ancestral archetypes, tribal elders or more personally – as 'the Grandfathers' for instance. Presences from the natural world – animals, birds or even something less specific – may also appear in a teaching role. But the questions any novice will want to ask their guide such as 'Who and what are you?' and 'Who and what am I?' will I think receive answers basically very similar to the ones that follow, however the connection is made. My own trains of thought and need for reassurance will hopefully also encourage others passing along the learning path.

Sîbclíus

Danger whip Ice-point
polished semi quavers
daggor
mottled visage
of old forest god
from Nordic drenched
wind,
petrifying small, yet acre eyes
to
unpulsed myopia

- pinescape feigning
a misted sun;

but wisdom-crack
lasers shaling ice
– wet
lichen grimace –
eavesdrop crescendo
to exploding leitmotifs,
heretic
rainbow sagas...

PG

26

Reading and Meditation

The Pupil – in conversation with Mist

I

What do you look like?
- *Mist.*
Are you an angel?
- *Perhaps.*
Are you my Guardian Angel, or Spirit Guide? Are there such things as Spirit Guides?
- *I am here to teach you, for you asked me to come. I was always there, but further from you.*
Are you 'Cassandra'? (DG: A previous source of channelled material)
- *No.*
Who is he/she?
- *Another.*
Are there more?
- *We are Legion.* (DG: I sensed reference here to the Bible and the story of the man possessed by devils, but meant in an explanatory manner suggesting many communicators not that this communicator was a devil.)
Have you a name?
  (No answer)
Are you the Goddess? (DG: I had had previous communications with a 'Goddess' source)
- *No.*
Did I know you in this life?
- *I knew you.*
Would I recognise you?
- *You already know me.*
(After some consideration, recalling the image of one of the teachers at the village school I attended when a child) Are

you Miss Lloyd?
- *(Smiles) Believe so if you will: you are again an infant and in the school for infants.*
Why must I learn? Do I have some mission?
- *You are the mission, o my dear child. (Emotion) You were thrown into the deep water and you have survived and shine forth with all the power we hoped for you.*
What are 'we'?
- *We are your own kind.*
Are there many?
- *We are legion.* (DG: This time a slightly different meaning, using the word more personally as an adjective)
How did I get here?
- *It was ordained.*
What must I do?
- *Be there and be your self.*
(After some thought) You are not Miss Lloyd, are you?
- *Miss Lloyd was within your childhood, which did not exist. Your memory was planted there, you have none only what has been permitted.*
Who are you, then?
- *It matters not. We are here. When you ask, one will come.*
Thank you.

II

(DG: *On this particular day it had been announced in the media that the world might be about to end soon as a result of collision with a comet so I tried to ask relevant questions. I have no idea whether the answers I was given were scientifically correct.*)

Can you tell me what is happening with the comet, please?
- *Very little. The fragments of the pattern are moving all the time like your kaleidoscope and one comet is nothing, less.*
But to us on the Earth?
- *Hope and life.*

Negativity can reverse.

Is this possible? Has anybody discovered it?

- *Does this matter? It happens.*

So the comet is not really important?

- *The smallest fragment is important equally as the greatest. But there is no comet in your mind. In the mind there is no movement, no collision.*

(After a moment) Why do I see the image of a snowflake, so beautiful and pure?

- *The perfection is mathematically the power of nought and yet it is infinity.*

What should I do about the comet?

- *Accept it.*

Will there be harm?

- *You will grow in reverse.*

Everyone else too?

- *In their ways.*

- *Rest and let go, for the heat nor the cold can harm you, nor the breaking of atoms or shattering of bone nor the mis-shapes of cell and bone. You will return to where you came and the silver and the mist of your kind. (Emotion, reassurance) Believe this, child, for we would never let you go so far alone nor abandon you. It was the images which confused you. You are of us and no thing can break or separate.*

Who are you?

- *We are your own kind. Rest, child, for we are with you.*

Am I a Star Child?

- *You are a child of light.*

III

Good evening to my teacher. Please tell me what you wish to teach me tonight.

- *Crystal water, a well, and there is a coral fish which swims into the depth and to the surface to whisper its message. You were a child then, and you are a child now, and must feel the water and listen to the fish*

Was this a past life?

- *There is only one life, one progression, child.*

I understand

I give you today the iris flower: its roots are long and never end. So the life in progressing along one root and surfacing again and again, for the flowers to bloom and spread their gloriousness, yet in the end, all the flowers are one.

I have heard today about something very advanced and powerful called kundalini. (DG: A form of yoga). What is kundalini, please?

- *(Smiles) It is what you will make of it.*

But different teachings all seem so complicated and to contradict each other, and they seem to me to get in the way of real understanding.

- *The bird does not need to study aerodynamics.*

I have felt I might have been a bird or some sort of spirit before.

- *Remember you tried to fly as a child? So your pet birds long for the freedom without their cage. (DG: I had two miniature doves.)*

If I let them loose, they would die.

- *Of course. Yet within they cannot use their wings.*

(I became upset) Is it cruel of me to keep them?

- *Without you they would die yet they aspire to be independent of you. With wings you would die yet you aspire to leave your human self. Do not ask too many questions, child.*

I feel I should ask deep questions, but I sense they would not be the right ones.

- *Look to the fountain, the water and the coral fish. Let the water of the pool speak.*

Was I a priestess? I feel I was some sort of oracle always.

- *You were aware of the need to serve.*

But why do I not like people, then? How can I overcome that?

- *Do not make assumptions on evidence which you do not possess. What is liking? You are not aware of liking. Wait until you can judge.*

judge. There is no need ~~to try. Simply be, to the ability~~ *which you are capable, and the rest will follow.*

I can see water flowing between the irises and the fish are darting among the ripples.

- *So all progresses, as you phrase it, you in the stream and the stream of its own volition, and the flowers bloom along the way, and yet all is one image in your mind.*

Are you really giving me these messages or are they already in my mind?

- *You are part of the great core of knowledge where all is revealed already. You know all, but it is clear to your sight fragment by fragment.*

Other people seem to have said everything I have to say.

- *Of course. All truth is the same.*

You make it sound so easy.

- *Why should it not be?*

All these teachings and regulations.

- *Look to the water and the fish. To each his own way. You studied the rules when other flowers bloomed for you, and wept at your ignorance. Now you move within the water like the coral fish and do not question how you swim.*

Why am I afraid of water?

- *Do not make assumptions.*

Did I drown?

- *At some time all men drown.*

But why am I afraid, please?

- *You fear only the power of the water to drown you.*

Will I drown in this life? How will I die?

- *(Smiles) You know the answer. Your heart will stop.*

(Again recalling my teachers at the village school) Are you Miss Lloyd? If not, are you Mr. Fisher?

- *Both.*

How can you be?

- *Because you recall us both.*

Are you a man or a woman?

Are you my ~~~ ~
- *One of them.*
You mean there are more?
- *All those above you are your higher selves, as you are their and our lower self.*
Are there any others like me? – with you, I mean. Us.
- *When you are aware of them, they will become parts of you.*
Will I meet them in this life?
- *That depends on yourself.*
Will I have to come back after this life?
- *That depends.*

Thank you.

Practical

1 Before any meditation or mindwork session, protect yourself with a prayer and accustom yourself to working within a sacred space you have cleansed and dedicated to whatever you perceive as the Source of life and light. Familiarise yourself with traditional methods (for instance, smudging) of cleansing and purifying both yourself and the areas around you; there are excellent instructive books available. Do not forget always to close mindwork sessions with a prayer of thanks.

2 Meditate on the words given to *The Pupil* in connection with yourself.

3 You may be already receiving guidance and instruction from a teacher or teachers but be aware too that teachings and messages from the spirit world can come in ways you might not have previously recognised. Look back over your life and try to identify any occasion when you might have encountered the voice of your guide or some personal communication from the natural or spirit world.

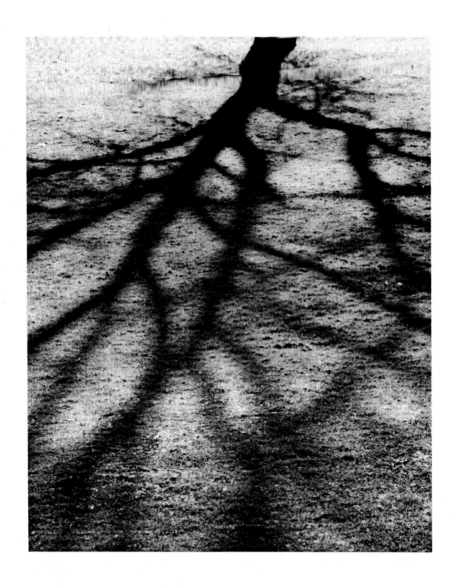

have myself of such age of twenty-two, I suffered a 'nervous breakdown' state of terrible trauma, cut my wrists with a razor blade. We are all more enlightened these days and realise that such acts are generally a 'cry for help' but apart from having been told I had committed a crime (as it was then) I was removed to the locked ward of the nearest psychiatric hospital, grimly referred to as 'the asylum'.

It happened a few days before Christmas, at a time when because the rest of the world seems to be enjoying the festive season, sufferers of depression and despair often feel worse than ever and the incidence of would-be suicides rises dramatically. I was at my lowest ebb when I came to myself sitting with bandaged wrists, weak and very shaky, in the window bay of the ward near the bed I had been assigned.

There was a small paved courtyard beyond. It was an extremely bitter winter that year and the few flowers and shrubs I could see were reduced to thinly straggling against the ravages of frost. The world was still and dead. But on one icy twig a robin was sitting a few feet from me beyond the glass and singing and somehow I felt something outside of myself take the burden I had found too heavy to carry and gently lift it.

The feeling did not last long of course, and it was a long struggle back to health and some semblance of sanity. Yet at that moment I knew I had taken the first tiny step out of the ward, the despair, the drugged misery. It was not that the robin spoke to me, nor any specific thing or voice, yet at that instant I was given a direct communication I have never forgotten. From where? From who or what?

The shaman does not ask such questions. The voice speaks and he listens.

Chapter 9

Night On the Bare Mountain

'You're sitting quietly in your yurt, minding your own business, when suddenly a hideous four-headed spirit monster blasts its way through the door flap, grabs you by the neck, yanks you up through the smoke-hole into some dreary realm where it proceeds to slap you around, rip you apart, dip you in a foul-smelling gook, staple you back together again and drop you back through the smoke-hole. Then it says, 'There! Now you're a shaman!'...

If that's the initiation into shamanism, who needs it?

Tom Cowan
Shamanism as a Spiritual Practice for Daily Life

Each has its place in the divine scheme. None of the darker experiences – dark to you, that is, because you do not like them – is so strong that you cannot overcome it. You will not be called upon in your earth life to face any test or crisis for which you do not possess the strength to overcome it...

Does growth not follow that which has been sown? Is not always this unchanging standard the divine pattern? The Great Spirit has not failed. The Great Spirit will not fail you if you allow the Great Spirit not to fail you.

Silver Birch

Since most of the shamans we ever hear about seem to be members of tribes who live far from the beaten paths of the West – often in other cultures and continents - our knowledge of the processes by which they achieve their role is necessarily limited. In spite of various accounts claiming to give details we have to assume that our knowledge of the training and preparation of a native shaman is largely hearsay, second-hand.

But some things we do know and one of these is that the shaman is always – inevitably, because he has to be – a person apart. To some degree he is always going to be isolated, different. Sometimes awareness of this apartness begins early, in many traditions the shaman being chosen, marked and trained from babyhood for his role or else receiving visionary confirmation of a vocation during childhood or – very commonly – during the onset of puberty. We can trace this practice of separateness back into antiquity for all communicants with Otherworlds, even the priests and priestesses at sacred shrines like Delphi, lived segregated from the community. Even when in consultation with the god (or goddess) on behalf of pilgrims seeking enlightenment, they had to be kept apart from the enquirers. The shaman has to keep apart from the world to whatever extent, not because he is better than everyone else but because he is more vulnerable.

It is no coincidence that many individuals gifted with this kind of awareness find it extremely difficult to exist as human beings and may suffer seeming 'breakdowns' or become affected to such a degree by the give and take of ordinary living that they cannot cope. It is difficult to say whether the painful experiences endured during such periods, when the individual seems to have removed from what everyone else accepts as reality, come first in order to establish necessary developments in the making of the shaman, or whether they happen incidentally because of the individual's particular and unique potential. In primitive tribes it was often accepted that the shaman - though a figure revered and of immense power and mystery, healer, priest, teacher might also be something of a liability on the community and need to be protected, taken care of and supported materially by the rest. Payment for spiritual services rendered could well have been in kind, in the form of food and shelter, warm clothing and provision of the physical necessaries of living.

The role of the shaman is not defined but is as it were universal, elemental. It cuts across all formal religions and faiths, and because the shaman is not necessarily a part of some established belief system (like a Christian or Buddhist monk, for example) he is likely to be very much unprotected, stripped of all defenses. The shaman is a creature out of its shell. Consequently, for this as well as other reasons, he is likely to recognise himself (even though it may not be apparent to others) by the fact that he will from a very early age have become accustomed to experiencing fear and learning how to deal with it. He is the ultimate 'sensitive' whose skin is so thin as to be almost non-existent; he is going to be throughout his earthly span of living intensely aware of the loneliness, isolation and fearful uncertainty that marks any spiritual quest or journey.

Show me any claimant to shamanic status, however charismatic, who does not admit to suffering a problem with his fears – even terrors – at times and I will not take him seriously. For though moments of intense ecstasy and bliss can be achieved and the Higher Worlds glimpsed, any kind of cthonic awareness means you cannot remain static and must move between all the worlds including the Lower. The mystic who walks surrounded in clouds of glory is not a shaman. The shaman knows he is never going to have that security of office well as the light.

In fact fear and terror are some of the tools the shaman learns to master and work with: they are marks of the true aspirant rather than signs of weakness. For what does terror teach us? That we can pass through it and survive. That we can both transcend it and cause it to be transcended. That terror as well as bliss are two sides of the same coin, each equally necessary and relevant to the fullness and completion of experience.

So often the true significance of the shaman's role – its hugeness of commitment and responsibility – is either not appreciated or else overlooked. Perhaps this is what I felt intuitively in my reactions to the 'wannabes' I encountered early on in my psychic career. I could not then understand how aspirants could lay such enormous significance on material trappings and displays of what looked like meaningless ritual, yet appear to lack genuine humility of spirit and be unaware of the deep personal sacrifice necessary in order to assume the authority of a true communicant with Otherworlds and representative of souls.

Even if one only begins conscious study later in life, awareness of the shaman's role is something that will overshadow every other aspect of that person's existence. It has to be vocational, destined, inevitable. Melanie Reinhart sums it up in these comprehensive terms:

'The typhonic (ie half animal, half human) mind and sensibility, and the shamanic initiation, are both characterised by a direct experience of the force-field lying beneath the myriad forms perceived by our senses...The shaman is one initially set apart from his or her tribe by the force and immediacy of personal religious experience and vision...Once having accepted his vocation, however, the shaman is highly regarded within his group...the shaman is the custodian of a heritage of direct access to realms of the spirit inaccessible to most people. '

The Initiation

For everything there has to be a starting point, a benchmark or reference, and enquirers are usually aware that there is some kind of initiation into shamanism though they may have no real idea of what this involves. It is generally accepted that by all accounts the initiation is not likely to be easy, involving as it does the symbolic 'shamanic death' from which the aspirant will emerge purified and reborn in new wisdom and awareness.

Most enquirers have a vague expectation of what lies ahead of them as they prepare to undergo such an initiation themselves, for this kind of test or trial can be found in all belief systems, in ancient myth and sacred symbolism. The step taken into the abyss in order to prove the initiate's fastness of resolve and courage in order to be accepted as worthy can take many forms - the walk through the valley of the shadow, the night spent on the bare mountain, the days fasting in the wilderness are all 'initiation' symbols and concepts.

Such tests might appear on the surface to be mainly of sheer physical endurance. A period of isolation and fasting in an unsupportive environment for any length of time would be difficult and frightening enough in itself, but the true shamanic initiation goes far beyond the physical. It involves undergoing awareness of an immense breadth of spiritual vision and connection by means of what has been called, 'an ecstatic journey to higher planes of consciousness'. In the words of Melanie Rheinhart: 'In every shamanic tradition, the candidate must undergo a period of intense psychological,

The general assumption made even by some of those who want to take courses in shamanism or live shamanic lives is that once the initiation has been passed – a kind of preparatory test, as it were - the worst is over. This could not be more wrong. The testing process is on-going and what seems initiation may well be simply marking some stage or development reached with further tests to come. There is not just one initiation but many for the whole journey is in itself nothing but an initiation. The sense of isolation and progression into a lonely wilderness can take years and indeed it may be this long, steadfast resolve and not the traumatic thunderbolts from heaven that will prove in the end to have been the real initiation. For it is often the keeping going that can be hardest, trying to cling to belief in what one is doing when there seems to be every reason for abandoning the way. The traditional torment of being 'torn apart by devils' too, may take half a lifetime or more before rebirth in new wisdom and awareness can even begin.

Yet conversely, initiation may not prove the terrifying experience people anticipate. This road is not always one of pain, and sometimes when a long period of trial has been humbly undergone, the spirit striving to learn from its experiences rather than bemoaning them, there can come the gift of a sudden, dazzling upsurge of light that lifts the soul on golden wings. If the trials are far more intense than anticipated, so too are the rewards, and glimpses like this of the bounty of the gods are jewels that will shine undimmed, prizes that put anything else one might achieve in life into insignificance.

The 'spontaneous signs of vocation' (in Reinhart's words) which might appear to form the shaman's initiatory test or trial may in a general sense happen involuntarily – at any age

- when some trauma occurs in the individual's life. The trauma is usually immense and often involves serious illness mental, physical or both, though as we have seen, the person involved might well always have seemed nervous, imaginative and extra sensitive. Sometimes a physical handicap or even a deformity is regarded as a special ability in this direction – people who suffered from epilepsy, for instance, or were born with other debilitating physical or mental conditions were long considered to have been touched by the gods.

Acceptance of the vocation is crucial. If it is denied or rejected the effects can cause damage both to the individual and the people around, though as with the time-span of initiation, even the struggle with acceptance of awareness can take far longer than people think.

Because the process is intensely personal and will vary with every individual, accounts of the different aspects of initiatory experience cannot adequately convey them, though there are many popular classic works available that describe and report such processes in locales that range from both North and South America to Africa to the countries of Siberia. It is up to the enquirer to make what he or she will from such records, and glean whatever they can that will be of significance or help to them personally.

The traditions of Native America provide inspiration for many. Richard Erdoes noted in his excellent study of the Plains Indians *The Sun Dance People* how 'The Plains Indian was a vision seeker. Dreams and images, seen only in his mind's eye, were his way of communicating with the Great Spirit.' When it was time for him to become a man, the young boy undertook a Vision Quest where he 'faced an ordeal of loneliness, hunger and thirst' in order to achieve enlightenment and be initiated into manhood. Chokecherry Gall Eagle noted in *Beyond the Lodge of the Sun*, his account of the traditional teachings of the Native American way:

would be taught, but first I would have a dream.'

John G. Neihardt (Flaming Rainbow) was the mouthpiece for the Lakota visionary Nicholas Black Elk, whose account of his shamanic experiences including his 'Great Vision' has long been one of the most accessible for the enquirer to study. Neihardt wrote in his Preface to the 1961 edition of his classic *Black Elk Speaks*:

'Finally the old man began talking about a vision that had come to him in his youth. It was his power-vision, as I learned later, and his fragmentary references to it were evidently only intended to arouse my curiosity, for he could not speak freely about a matter so sacred before the assembled company. It was like half seeing, half sensing a strange and beautiful landscape by brief flashes of sheet lightning.'

It is words like these that stir the soul of the aspirant. An awareness of spiritual vocation prompts the need to isolate oneself and go consciously apart whether physically or mentally. During a period of preparation and initiatory meditation one begins to 'wrestle with one's demons' in the struggle not only to find oneself but to free oneself from that self. It will become apparent during this period of self-examination and revelation however, that by the same paradox we have already noted, it is not necessarily the commencement of the shamanic journey that draws the novice into lonely places so he can seek communion with the spirits, and endeavour through fasting and hardship to break through the barriers of flesh and soar with the elements into other worlds. The way of the shaman has no beginning and no end: though one may have been aware of a starting-point the journey will prove later to have had a quite different beginning - indeed to have been on-going all the time.

Don Jose Matsuwa and his wife Dona Josefa Medrano, described in Steven McFadden's *Profiles of Wisdom* as 'singing shamans, healers and master ceremonial leaders' of their people, Huichol Indians of the Sierra Madre mountains of western Mexico, revealed to the author at the ages of 110 and 96 years old respectively how they had achieved their shamans' roles. Don Jose, McFadden reported, began to study the shaman's path in his early thirties, absorbing and learning from the natural world: '... for ten years he lived alone in a cave or in the forest, praying and studying in the school of the spirit...Altogether, he says, his shamanic apprenticeship spanned sixty-four years, during which he fasted many times, including one stretch while he was on Vision Quest when he went for fifteen days without food and water.'

Huichol women may become shamans by studying and training in the same way as men and this is typical of most cultures. Women were allowed to become Druids among the pre-Christian Celts (a process that took at least twenty years) and though the popular belief is that the 'medicine men' of Native American Indians were generally men, women could also become noted medicine women and healers.

The chosen successor to Don Jose was his adopted grandson Brant Secunda, born in New York, who though not an Indian, was led to the Huichols by the kind of intuitive spiritual guidance that makes the story – as all such stories of this kind are inclined to - sound like fiction. He told McFadden that he spent years with Don Jose being instructed in the role he was destined to fulfil, and worked two apprenticeships of six years each in order to learn how to become first a healing shaman and then a singing or ceremonial shaman. Reading this account I personally found that one particular comment from Brant Secunda hit home like a lightning bolt.

What an awesome, what a terrifying job description. Yet what a position to aspire to, what a privilege beyond all imagining if it could be attained or even glimpsed. And if achieved – to however a limited an extent – then surely a role to die for.

Speaking Personally

Someone reading through my promotional leaflet at a Psychic Fair the other day asked me with a quite genuine curiosity: 'How did you know you were born a Celtic Wise Woman?'

I was able to tell her candidly that I had not known anything of the sort, that I had not had a clue; that in fact the first forty-odd years of my life had been spent with a history of breakdowns and illness diagnosed as caused by 'manic depression' or even 'Multiple Personality Disorder' among other things; that though I was recognised as being extremely gifted intellectually, a very individual and talented writer, so far as my personal life was concerned I had been very much a square peg trying to fit myself into a series of round holes. Nobody seemed able to tell me whether I was an eccentric genius or simply a sad case who had completely lost the plot.

As for the 'label', I explained that I had written a book called *Celtic Wise Woman* about my psychic and healing work which set it against my Welsh country heritage and background, adding that: 'The description – any description of this kind - is just a form of words. I don't know if that is really what I am but it seems as good a way as any to convey the essence of what I do and represent to other people.'

Looking back, particularly regarding initiatory experiences of whatever kind, I think the most significant thing for me is that I can never remember a time when I was not in a very intimate, spiritual way afraid, though I had no conscious idea why. Once becoming aware of my psychic gifts and potential, I can now explain some of this fear away by saying that obviously, as an extremely aware sensitive – a 'wise child' I had 'picked up' much of the fear and negative feelings of those around me. Another source of threat was probably the Welsh Methodism I was brought up in with its heavy bias towards sin, repentance, guilt and shame. But even these do not explain the vivid incidents of extreme and overwhelming psychic trauma I experienced as a child which remained permanently imprinted in my mind.

I never spoke of them to anyone. Not only did I not know how to put them into words but I intuitively felt they were mysterious, forbidden 'adult' things I would not have been supposed to know about or meddle with, sensing even then, that I was treading on dangerous ground. In later years I was inclined to dismiss the memories, assuming that every young child probably suffered similar experiences and that others might well have coped with them better than I had done. It is only in the context of the kind of spiritual development I am now familiar with and work with, that they take on their proper perspectives.

Once, aged about six, I missed a bus that would take me home from a music lesson one evening, and walked the miles along the country road home in the November darkness: nothing special about that since we all, as country children, often walked long distances alone. Yet on that occasion I was in such a state of nervous terror and shock when I eventually stumbled into the welcome light of the first street lamp in the village, that it took me some time to recover. I had encountered no physical person on the way but had experienced something I would always remember afterwards even though I could not have described it. I had been spiritually challenged, tested against the power of the dark, pushed to the limits of my endurance and beyond and been

On another occasion perhaps a year later, I remember making my first conscious communication with Otherworlds – daring to speak directly to both the world of angels and the world of demons and darkness. I was in my small bedroom at home, supposed to be asleep but (as I so often was as a child) lying awake and aware, tensed in every muscle. I cannot say what prompted the faltering mental communications since I had never heard anything about the ways of shamans, psychics or magical practices at that time but the result was that my room dissolved into another dimension and the space filled with such immense powerful energies that I was knocked to the floor, where I crouched cowering and trying desperately to keep a grip on my sanity. Even the angelic power was terrifying – the demons were indescribable - and the whole overwhelming experience was such that I took great care never to open my mind to anything like it again for a very long time. I felt once more that I had had to pass through some immense and terrible trial and that I had been lucky to survive.

It is only when looking back that the patterns of development become visible. Much later – in my mid-forties - I underwent another, more definitive experience so earth-shattering that I felt I emerged from it a new and trembling spirit, shaking off as it were, the mental blood and slime of rebirth. The setting was not some high mountain peak or wilderness, it was during a three-year period when I lived in North London (though not in the flat I later occupied during my 'London years'). Finding myself on the point of complete breakdown, wanting to try and 'end it all', I retreated instead, hardly able to eat or sleep, deep into myself and into whatever realms presented themselves. I made an intense inner voyage over a period of some eight weeks in virtual isolation recording my thoughts and feelings day by day. Years later I was able to will...' This journey, taken in great fear and anguish of spirit was, I think now, a journey of initiation,,.'

My account of those traumatic weeks was later published as *Putting My Selves Together*. I knew it had been a monumental turning-point for me personally, yet at the time and for many years afterwards I had no real awareness of what might have been taking place in any spiritual, psychic or shamanic sense. It is only glancing down some of the discarded opening pages now, setting the words I had scribbled as an expression (I thought then) of weakness and failure into the context of this chapter, that I can more fully understand and interpret those desperate wails from the depths of isolation and despair as a plea for recognition, for identity. Other aspirants on the shamanic path may recognise themselves here:

'...I can't meet people on an equal footing...I may horrify new acquaintances by revealing some sign of weakness, of the fact that I'm not like them, not stable and well-balanced like everyone else. I may crack; something may prove too much; I might want something they can't give...They will realise then just how inferior a person I am, how lacking, how riddled with doubts and terrors, how preoccupied with trying to see my way forward, trying to cope with the pain of the past and the unbearable difficulty of the present, afraid of the future...

'Sometimes I wonder just how much struggle the brain can take. I mentioned it to my doctor a few weeks ago, and she told me to think of what concentration camp victims endured and came through. The human mind can stand a lot. So now I'm doubly shamed because I am not a concentration camp victim with a reason for my difficulties...

'I have become resigned to the fact that no-one will ever really know me, the real me with the good and bad things,

understand. Perhaps that's what I am... form of communication I can't find. But I seem to live among strangers; everyone I meet in the future will be a stranger to me and I will never be accepted for what I really am, the person who is me...*

'I have to try and keep justifying my actions...And I don't want to have to keep feeling obligated to justify my existence. We can't all behave like text-book prototypes, you press a button and we do the right thing. But I feel that nobody will ever accept me now without surprise and probably disapproval, since I am very conscious that in the past, I failed.*

'The thing to do, of course, is to wipe it all out, never mention the past, face the future with a blank behind me. But the me I am now is a direct result of those past years, and even if I could wipe them out I would be wiping myself away. The child, the girl, the young woman I was are all part of me, all of us searching for something – I don't know what – until in the end, hopefully, we find some sort of peace.'*

This was not the first journey of a similar kind that I had been forced to make. Years earlier when aged about thirty, I had undergone a similar trauma though I had not been able to keep a record of it. So far as I knew, everyone felt at the time that it was nothing more than a severe 'mental breakdown' of the sort I had experienced to varying degrees since late adolescence. I was confined to a psychiatric unit for some four or five months where I underwent various kinds of treatment and afterwards spent three years at the home of my parents. I could not possibly have coped alone since I was, as I could only describe afterwards, 'similar to a vegetable', unable to relate to anyone or communicate with them. The days were spent in a condition of complete withdrawal where I hardly spoke or moved, I fell into untantonio sleep states at all times of the day, simply collapsing into oblivion.

None of the medical practitioners who were consulted seemed to be able to give a diagnosis and we never found any explanation. Nothing seemed to have happened to me to bring such a violent reaction about, yet I was displaying all the symptoms of chronic trauma. While confined to the psychiatric unit, I found I had lost the ability to read and could not make sense of even one line or sentence. I was unable to write since the muscles of my hands could not grasp a pen. And for some weeks I was also literally unable to speak, my vocal chords being, I suppose, paralysed so that all I could utter was a hoarse croak. The sense of alienation (referred to by all for the sake of convenience as 'depression') was so horrendous that the only way I could ever describe it was as though I was at the bottom of an intensely deep, narrow pit, a shaft or well, completely in blackness, completely alone. Somewhere far above I could from time to time just hear vague sounds, just glimpse a tiny twinkle of light like a star. I had to climb the sheer walls of the black pit to get out and reach that light: the effort took me long, long months. Nearly three years.

The lesson to be learned from all this is that the wilderness, the bare mountain peak, the 'dreary realm' of demons and spirit monsters can in fact be found anywhere. My own experience of incarceration in an asylum for the insane probably had exactly the same result in the end as if I had travelled to find enlightenment in the wilds of Tibet or withdrawn into the Arizona desert on a 'Vision Quest' – I either had to emerge from it empowered, or allow myself to be lost for good.

Eyes shaded
Against the sun-spanned rage
- bronze, purple, gold –
That roars across the autumn valley,
I gaze from this fiery ridge
On seagulls playing statues
On distant balustrades.
The others bustle
Love-play and choruses,
Trapped unaware by landlocked tides,
Uncosmic-felt divinity,
Or squabble
White against brown-earthed fields,
Once haunting cries
Pruned now
To bare inessentials.

I call back hoarsely,
Flap my unseagulled wings
- my tide run out –
And soar to an unknown bliss
And the terrifying stars.

PG

sharing of activities or even mixing with others. It need not and should not be a lonely path but certainly one of exclusiveness.
There is the certainty of discovering one's inner self by following that loner path and there is wisdom to be attained in so doing. But, as this quotation about The Hermit reminds us, 'Be humble, if thou wouldst attain wisdom; be humbler still when wisdom thou hast mastered'.
...(in) the words of the Buddha spoken long ago, 'The light of truth's high noon is not for tender leaves!'

John Christopher Travis,
writing in *Prediction* magazine
on the Tarot cards The Hermit and Strength

The main problems that arise for the novice concern the sustaining of belief in his sense of vocation, in himself and in the role – unspecified often and undefined – that he now finds himself trying to carry out. It is the day by day uncertainties not only of how to cope, but of whether he is proceeding in the 'right' direction along what must be a very personal path, that will exhaust and absorb his energies rather than traumas involved with spiritual or mystical enlightenment.

Anyone who follows any kind of spiritual vocation will be well aware of the grinding power of such uncertainty to reduce one seemingly to nothing. Tests of faith and vocational crises become almost constant occurrences, whether within recognised disciplines or outside of them. Thomas Merton, a Trappist monk, has been described as 'one of the greatest spiritual masters of the Twentieth Century'. He had been a member of the community at the Abbey of Gethsemani, Kentucky, for over ten years when he wrote in his journal for

'?? October 1950: 'Throu my retreat I have been having another one of those nervous breakdowns. The same old familiar business. I am getting used to it now since the old days in 1936, when I thought I was going to crack up on the Long Island Railroad, and the more recent one since Ordination. Now this.'

An increasing awareness of some kind of higher destiny and power bestowed brings with it an increasing sense of doubt, isolation and apprehension, as faith and trust has to be placed entirely in the sole reality and truth of the novice's guides and instructors. The process, necessarily involving the complete surrender of self – even though willingly, perhaps eagerly assumed and accepted - is truly awful (in the sense of 'filled with awe', though it may be in a terrifying sense also) and takes immense courage.

As I struggled with my own visions and impressions to try and identify my true self, I increasingly found it difficult to believe in the reality of the images presented to me. I felt

stripping away of the mask – or else the assumption of one might appear empowering and yet the sense may well be of complete helplessness. Surrender to the Higher Self, whatever form this takes, must be utter and complete and all former defenses have to be let go, all former weapons laid down. The self dies and what is reborn has to be accepted unquestioningly, with no desires and no expressions of personal want or need.

In the early months of my own conscious working with Spirit, I conducted written 'conversations' with Mist whenever I needed advice or reassurance, often on an everyday basis. Though I thought I was being prompted by a need to try and find my way forward, it is obvious that my real need was simply for help to cope on a mundane level. There is often some outward physical manifestation in the novice of the huge mental effort that is being made at times like this. It can take the form of unaccountable skin rashes, mouth ulcers, digestive problems or similar symptoms of stress – all of which I had suffered from for years - but for me the effort now began to make itself manifest in other ways that were frightening and disabling: severe panic attacks and heart palpitations as well as the more usual depressions, anxieties and 'personality difficulties'.

Every person's initiatory experiences, their fears and consequently their demons and the trials that result from trying to confront those demons, are different. Some of my early conversations held with Mist are given below. They indicate how intense as well as how universal is the novice's fear and sense of bewilderment and inadequacy, how great is his need for a guide.

Reading and Meditation

Holding on - In conversation with Mist

I

Why am I here?
- *You are needed.*
How can my suffering be of any use?
- *How do you know you suffer?*
Because I can feel the pain. Because I carry the weight of longing for my home.
- *Your home is with you.*
You mean I should be more cheerful, make the best of things?
- *Count your blessings?* (Smiles)
I am so tired.
- *Those who do nothing are far more tired than those who work.*
I have heard this before.
Why am I needed?
- *Even one star would be missed.*
There's such a lot of negativity.
- *That is why you are needed.*
I don't know what to do.
- *Shine. Be.*
Can you help me?
- *At great distance nothing matters. All stars are specks of light, points. Let them be so.*
Thank you.

II

My teacher be near me.
- *I am here.*
What is happening?
- *Weakness.*
But whose? And why now?

Yes, that is so. Thank you.
- *Do not try to know.*
I feel such a fool. And on all sides there is hurt and laughing.
- *Back to childhood? (Smiles)*
Yes, so right. (I always felt 'different' when at school)
- *You are not a child only of light. You are a spirit of elevated wisdom. Do not compare or contrast. There is none.*

III

(Feeling the spirits were prompting me, I had travelled alone to Ireland feeling so ill I seriously wondered whether I would make the journey, but determined to 'die living' if I had to. My fellow travellers on the plane might have been ancient pagan warriors by their terrifying aspect, noise and presence. They turned out to be Welsh rugby supporters!)

Mist my love, my darling, are you with me?
- *In the air, Kathleen, every breath. (By this time I thought of Mist in terms of great intimacy. The name 'Kathleen' was simply a reference to the fact that I was in another country. The name Mist had given me which 'he' habitually used to address me, is discussed elsewhere)*
I am unsteady but I know this is the right way.
- *Assuredly, among the warriors, your eve before the battle, my brave girl. They are rough but do also search the Grail.*
I know, Mist. Help me.
- *Your cloak is your protection. Walk without fear. You are known and recognised.*
I did not expect this (suffering and terror and testing)
- *Did your bird know the cage?*
Give me enough strength.
- *Take it, do not struggle alone. It is not necessary.*
I am not sure how to.
- *Rest, my dove, do not fear the clipping of wings, the hunter's*

57

snare.

Have I the strength?
- *There is an easy way. Do not fight the air, the mist, it gives you life. You know the dungeon, accept freedom. The dark is no more than the light with pain. You are not alone. Loose the thorn and embrace the rose sisterhood. It is all the same.*
It hurts.
- *Do you need me to teach you that? But what is hurt only joy gone wrong. Too much joy perhaps – snow can kill as well as fire. There is nothing wrong unless you make it so.*
Thank you.

IV

Mist my love my darling, my shield and far-off hope, why do I have all this pain, mental and physical?
- *Why not?*
But the books say I create it all and I do not think so. I cannot escape from it.
- *Then take it my dear girl and carry it, you do so for a good reason.*
Should I feel ashamed that I create it?
- *You have nothing within you of which to be ashamed. All that needs be shamed is without, clinging on.*
I feel I have failed in every way possible.
- *Your feelings are not facts. Just shine, be, for all is between you and the light. You will reflect like a mirror. The blemishes are not on the mirror itself. Find yourself, dear girl, reflect, do not look at the debris cluttering the mirror's surface. Hold to the light only. Other reflections are meaningless.*
Should I be proud or is that a sin?
- *Where light is, there is no sin. You will be punished enough, you do not need to punish yourself.*
What about my situation? (Regarding the difficult relationship I was in at that time and trying to summon the courage to leave it)
- *Reflect.*

58

feelings. They do not matter, ... debris.
Thank you.

Practical Work

1 Look back over your own experience. Has there been any difficult period or incident you might be able to interpret as a form of spiritual initiation in the light of what has been discussed in this chapter, wherever it might have taken place?

2 Has there been any transcendent or otherwise emotional experience you could interpret in a similar way?

3 Consider *In conversation with Mist* above and apply what has been said about uncertainty, inadequacy and difficulty in coping or keeping going to yourself.

4 Though most shamanic experience, as we have seen, is difficult to describe and is traditionally handed down verbally, begin now the habit of examining and considering the events of your life and making notes on your spiritual progress. Keep a record of your spiritual journey in a book kept especially for this purpose, making regular entries. As well as your own thoughts, feelings and inspirational writing, include any sayings, quotes or comments from other sources which have particularly inspired or spoken to you.

Urban Empowerment: Finding Sacred Space

Sanctuary

Conical lines now yawn
And dip,
Holding in the speckled bird
Of recollection
By tangled branches.

Tomorrow, the gardeners
Will come –
Tying the undisciplined yew
Back into symmetry.

But from between
Wire hoops,
None will hear
The daytime throb
Of the speckled bird,
Ragamuffined
By twilight fears.

PG

All true wisdom is only found far from men, out in the great solitude...

The shaman Igjugarjuk

But it is the unintentionally wild places which now provide habitats for most of London's wildlife. Derelict railway depots, disused water-works, Victorian cemeteries, railway embankments and even the roofs of buildings provide new urban habitats. Kestrels nest on city centre office blocks, herons fish in the Royal Parks, and foxes regularly raise cubs on wasteland within a stone's throw of the Old Vic Theatre. Wildlife is there but not by design.'

Bob Smyth
The Green Guide to Urban Wildlife

Traditionally, the vision quest is followed in empty, wild places, in the secret citadels of nature far from the habitations of man. In Brant Secunda's words: 'To become empowered as a shaman, you have to go where there is power...You give a prayer and an offering to the place of power, and you get to harvest the power of that place.' So how does all this relate to the city dweller, when the city is generally regarded as somewhere to run away from rather than run to?

Dick Whittington famously discovered his potential when he heard the Bow Bells chime out the message 'Turn again, Whittington, Lord Mayor of London', but most people who are trying to 'find themselves' in a spiritual sense do not see any connection between their earnest quest and high-rise flats, or mile after mile of sprawling suburb. Traditionally the city is very much a material place, a place where dreams of pavements of gold are shattered and humanity can be forced to descend to the lowest depths of degradation. It is a place of illusion, setting for some of the most spectacular palaces of mammon.

So can it be possible to 'be yourself' or magically invoke other selves to the accompaniment of police sirens; or in the chaos and crush of rush hour on the Underground, to connect with your spiritual, astral or etheric bodies; to find other worlds while sitting on the top of a red London bus? Can the

And what about connecting with the natural world? Indigenous peoples with shamanic traditions lived close to their animals. The Comanche, for instance, were so uncannily attached to their horses that when the Frontier artist George Catlin was studying their ways during the 1830s, he wrote that though he considered them 'homely', as soon as one of the tribe 'lays his hand upon his horse, his face, even, becomes handsome, and he gracefully flies away like a different being.'

Animals have always been closely related to humans and important to them. Research indicates that many religions have long-standing beliefs in metempsychosis and transmigration of souls from/into animal form, even of life as plants or stones. But what if one is more drawn to shopping than smallholding, more at home in Oxford Street than down on the farm? How does the aspiring shaman investigate the worlds of nature within the confines of the city? Would it not after all be more honest, more truthful, to seek yourself in some place apart – go to the wild, to the open country, where the heart of life beats as it has always done in the old, slow measure of the seasons and the days, where all is fateful in its inevitability?

I never had a problem with such dichotomies. So far as discovering or expressing one's true self is concerned, I found that experiments with nonconformity and individuality expressed in extremes of dress or mannerism are far more likely to pass without comment in the city than in the wide open spaces of the countryside. The city in this respect is far more accommodating, far more flexible, more tolerant and more willing to extend its mental horizons.

I came to know and love the closely built streets of London as physically inspiring as soul-uplifting to me as rocky prospects and mountain views might be to those who seek their inspiration in the countryside. To me, the city is representative of man's various strivings and aspirations towards meaning, towards form and shape.

I found immense natural beauty in the patterns and colours of railings, pavements, streetlights in the rain; I saw magic in the silhouettes of bridges and high buildings against the dawn sky, the Embankment reflected in the Thames at midnight. Shapes, patterns do not have to be formed by 'natural' growths such as rocks or trees. The reflections of the city - an old wrought iron lamp's night shadow, or even something we might regard as a 'blot on the landscape' like the stark panorama of cranes, rooftops or the scars of dereliction – can all be viewed as expressions of meaning through the eyes of an artist, a poet or a shaman, who bring the awareness of other worlds to their perceptions of this one.

I found the extremes of the city equally inspirational. Life does not teach us to expect only brightness and pleasure. Consciousness of the balance between light and shadow is what brings maturity, and the ability to appreciate the gifts offered by the darker aspect of existence. Perhaps because the shams and illusions of the city are in their way just as honest as the apparent 'naturalness' of places removed from man's busy metropolis, they offer just as great an opportunity – possibly a greater one – to be able to 'discover yourself'. Connect with the source of your being. Identify who and what you really are.

And as for the natural world, city dwellers can have just as strong an identification with animals, plants, growing things. City cats and dogs are passionately appreciated, not only for themselves and perhaps because they represent that spiritual connection, but because their owners have to make more of an every tiny garden and window box, every new branch budding on a bush, every tree hungrily recognised and loved in a much more immediate way than if surrounded by the glorious bounty of the open country.

I have mentioned already that for me assumptions are there to be challenged. The instruction I received personally concerning initiation and the sacred space in which it could occur, came from a source that on the surface appeared to have little to do with shamans and shamanic awareness. The mentor who 'came through' for me was not the medicine man of a lost tribe, but an unassuming English monk who had spent his life worshipping his God as a Christian brother.

This was how I described my initial encounter with him in my book *In and Out the Windows*:

'Drenched with sunlight in the landscape of 12th century England, an old monk sits in his garden where the scents of herbs, bitter and pungent, rise on the golden air. He nods, half-asleep, the abbey walls dreaming darkly behind him...I first became aware of the presence of the old monk and the image of his garden in 1997 in the unexpected setting of a coffee shop in the King's Road, London. While drinking my coffee and waiting for a friend I felt impelled to scribble down some sentences that seemed to be in the process of dictation within my head though I did not know where they were coming from. It was only after several days...that my mental image clarified itself and I discovered I had made contact with Brother Gregory, an Augustinian monk who had lived in the late 1100s somewhere in the South of England.'

In fact there was more to the story than that. My contact with Brother Gregory actually came about as a result, once again, of a specific request I had sent out to the spirits, for though I trusted Mist to guide me spiritually, I was very conscious of the lack of a physical teacher (a psychic 'personal trainer' if you like). Looking for something that provided a complete philosophy for training oneself to live by, I had been trying to study a manual on martial arts that provided a rigorous discipline that would be physical as well as mental. I felt at the time that perhaps I was not subjecting myself to enough physical challenge – or even the deprivations advocated by various regimes in order to achieve spiritual enlightenment - but I soon realised that physically, such a regime was far beyond my limitations.

So once again the traditional way did not seem the right one for me, yet I still felt the need for some sort of discipline, and asked the spirits if I might be given instructions, rules to live by, from somewhere else. I hoped as I had previously hoped before I made contact with Mist, that the result (wherever it eventually arrived from) would provide a kind of authoritative reference work tailored to my particular need.

When the first communications came they seemed to bear no resemblance to anything I might have expected. Interesting yes, but hardly important or relevant, especially when I discovered my communicant was not a physically powerful man. He was old and frail, and regarding mental power too, he had been the humblest of monks – possibly even a lay-

instructions and see that they provided me with exactly what I had asked for. It took a long time to realise that an unlettered old man steeped in Christianity, who had probably never stepped far beyond his abbey walls much less sought the desert, the wilderness or the high mountain in a physical sense, could reveal all I needed to know about the landscapes, the places of power where the aspirant might experience initiatory visions.

Brother Gregory taught me to see how the sacred space of the shaman may be created in words, in images that need have nothing to do with the physical wilderness, desert or jungle. Each creates the shamanic landscape from his own familiar experience and for a person like me, brought up in the tradition of 'Sunday worship', access to the bright worlds may be found within the blessed walls of any church building. It does not have to be some ancient country sanctuary, even some soaring cathedral within the urban setting. It can be any church. And though my mentor was a Christian, the church can be of any faith. The urban shaman need never feel he walks comfortless, for the voice of a companion is always there if he should seek it out.

Even more importantly, I had learned that any place can become sacred space, even if it is a coffee shop or a one-room city flat. And the brother had also advised me wisely on the subject of martial arts and physical discipline. In my own case, I had done enough physical suffering. There was no need to lose myself further in the deprivations of the body, I must learn to carry my own particular scars and be content with my body's limitations. Each in his own way finds his own wilderness and is subjected to the trials appropriate for him as a novice. Sometimes it is harder to acknowledge one's limitations than blindly force oneself beyond the pain barrier.

Mindwork

Reading and meditation

Brother Gregory's early messages are given below, just as they came to me. I did not, as I have said, immediately appreciate their significance and originally assumed they were intended as messages for my then partner Paul (now my husband) who is a horticulturist. It was only later that I realised how universal was their scope, as well as the great depth of their wisdom.

Instruction - teachings of Brother Gregory

I

There is movement with no movement, and so all movements can be made with no participation of the body. You can cover oceans and rise above the flight of eagles and never open your eyes.

Conserve does not mean save, it means intensify by stillness so that one arm is the arm of ten thousand of your army.

There are no rules, the discipline is one to which you will come of your own volition. Do not refuse to live in mistake for concentration upon God; your life was given as life not death. Life in all ways flows and moves and is liquid; the stagnant pool rotting in its own filth is a dark world of gases and a light that is not the sun nor yet the moon. The creatures of that world belong there, you do not.

achieved and within which all is balanced. So you too must bridge the world of the body and the world of the spirit, passing from the earth to the air and beyond; yet the plant does not move but its inexorable force can break through the rock or a barrier placed above it to reach the light.

How does the plant know where it is to go and why does it persist in its struggle for growth? There is within something you might call a 'programme' but a plant is not artificially created, it is born of the vibrant life force and the birth and death of a flower, even a weed (for there are no weeds), causes the universe to mourn as for the piled bodies of a war. Everything is relative and the life of a flower or a plant contributes as much to the well-being and harmony of the cosmos as one man's crucifixion. In their way the plants are allies who will give you secure rest when you are weary, love and cherishing when the day is a long and lonely one; they are your brothers and sisters, guiding you on with their flaming robes of colour and giving you strength. Take it freely, for it is there.

Eat and drink sparingly of all that sustains you, even the glory of the vision. The vision beckons like a great lake with a banquet outspread upon the sward beside it. The desperate will leap into the water and submerge themselves and yet when they come forth they have not tasted even a drop of it upon their mouths. They run through the banquet feast trying to lift everything at once and cram full their lips, and in the end a few crumbs remain with them.

Taste sparingly and the small cup of water is more than enough, the fragment of bread is food for a week's journey. Again it is relative, there is always enough, but for those whose greed is uncurtailed there will be less than nothing.

What is morning? A lightening and a lifting, and after the chaos of darkness, fear and doubt, the delicate shapes of the landscape take on their true perspective. We walk in many landscapes my son, but the true landscape you will know for it is always the same and is never shaken by outside circumstance even though it changes subtly like something seen through a mist or the heat haze of high summer.

The water below the mill may twindle to a thread and the beasts seek shade and lie as though they await death but the blue of the horizon is constant as the colour of the madonna's robe. Even when the sun is down the horizon is still there and your foot will be aware of the way. The doubts which beset you will change the road you know to a path that wanders across the thin coarse grass into nothing and nowhere. The dark cannot touch you so long as you do not allow it to take your feet from the road you know, but then it will have you.

From the top of the cliff or the body hanging in the wood or rising bloated in the green depths of the quarry pool, these are the results not of mistakes or failings but of fear that let their uneasy feet leave the path, the pedlar promising gold, the wide-eyed girl with white skin beneath her torn robe.

Have faith, my son, have the faith to hold and not to doubt what you know to be the truth however the other seems to have come from the hand of God. And have patience to wait out the urgency and the fear of loss. Around you there are quivering spirits which have grasped branches that have bent and will not take their weight, that have straddled stepping stones too far apart. You are yourself and have found your way forward.

and the blue of your mantle looked for by eyes that have watched a long time. My dear son in this bright dawn, you are a glory like the golden light to eyes faded and old.

IV

The landscape is calm, my son, but it will not be always so. Even as you accept the powers and allow your spirit to rise and soar so that you are one with God and will never again be the clay, untouched, you will see beyond, like an echo, the landscape of winter, where all the life is dead and there is no God.

These are the same, there is no difference between them and if you will see that, you will see with the eyes of God himself, for God is within; and whether your hand reaches out to touch the sores of leprosy or the skin of the face that is turned to you softly in love, so God is there and you will touch him and he will touch you, and it must be so for this is the law by which you are bound.

And many times you will have heard voices in the dusk and been unaware of their meaning, and have been held between the two worlds because it was not the time, but now my son, it is the time, and the powers are in your hands and you have accepted them in joyfulness and resignation and set yourself apart.

Oh my dear son I have thought many times of this day, but my senses are dumb and I cannot speak, and this too is the law, for you come before me in the morning of your flowering and I am blind and old, and your radiance dazzles me to nothing.

Forgive me. I too have my place, yet even the sky weeps dew at the coming of the dawn.

Ave accebatum illustrium fortuibus selectum regne. Gloria, gloria in mundi.

Practical

1 Study Brother Gregory's teachings and apply them to your own experience.

Notice how the Brother has touched on many recognisably shamanic concepts while using the language he was familiar with – spiritual journeying, spiritual discipline, vocational awareness, terror of other realms, universality of existence.

2 Visit city churches of all creeds, sit quietly and open yourself to whatever experience you are to be given without prejudice or expectation.

3 Visit any other places you feel drawn to, including museums or libraries where you may discover accounts of sacred landscapes and initiatory journeying from different cultures.

4 Investigate the green spaces, parks and animal sanctuaries within the urban environment and find how extensive is the connection with the natural world. I no longer live in London, for instance, but on a recent visit, on a twenty-minute journey on the train to Epsom, I saw three foxes – three more than I have encountered in the last six months in the Staffordshire Moorland area which is now my home.

Chapter 4

The Entertainer

I am large, I contain multitudes

Walt Whitman
Leaves of Grass

...he existed in a social limbo...in...scenes of court life he occupies otherwise empty spaces or is shown flitting from one group of courtiers to another, a barely corporeal presence

John Southworth
Fools and Jesters at the English Court

Watching Peter Hall's work with masks over the past twenty years I have realised that the mask can affect the body and vice versa. At times watching the recent ten-hour epic Tantalus *I became convinced that a static mask could metamorphose as the emotional journey developed within the work.*

Stewart McGill
Writing in *Dance Expression* magazine

The shaman embodies the paradox of the Wise Fool that in various guises has appeared throughout history and often played an important role. The jester with his cap and bells who alone in a king's court was allowed to speak the truth, and yet who had to conceal his wisdom beneath the flippancy of a buffoon, was often one of the most powerful influences in the kingdom. Shakespeare's 'Fools' are familiar examples. Their lines and songs contain some of the most profound statements in his plays.

Ancient Greek Drama and the masks of the theatrical performers. The 'comedian' of classical theatre was the antithesis of the tragedian: the masked ranks of the Chorus, who spoke with one voice, can perhaps be found to have metamorphosed into the 'Fool', the 'nebulo' of European history, the 'nobody' who stood outside of society and had no recognised standing. The same anonymous figure might also represent the god. Shadowy shapes would speak from behind a mask in the voice of the god at shrines and oracles.

These inspired, almost divine 'comic' or 'grotesque' figure can be found in many cultures, for the Fool is often represented as ugly, flawed, even repulsive. Court Fools of history were sometimes mentally impaired, the popularly named 'idiots' or 'innocents' who nevertheless were able to see truth and speak it without the subterfuges of the apparently more sophisticated.

Pierrot in the Commedia dell' Arte is Everyman, the Tearful Wise Fool, the wanderer whose country is the Moon. The entertainer/Wise Fool aspect of the shaman provides him with many roles, among them performer, dancer, mime, narrator or commentator (the role played by the Chorus of Ancient Greek drama). He may be a folk singer or a storyteller. Black Elk describes the performance of the Horse Dance, carried out in order to teach his people and to acquaint them the content with his visions. He also tells of the heyokas, 'sacred fools' who performed doing everything wrongly and back-to-front in order to make the people laugh when times were bad. The clowns of tradition, as we have already seen, do the same. The shaman was the original buffoon, the original entertainer. He had a role to carry out that no other member of his tribe could have fulfiled.

On one level a shaman is an anonymous character who acts out the dramas of our lives and helps us to understand them and cope with them. The funeral mutes, the mummers of mediaeval times, the entertainers at a wedding, the Morris dancers of the traditional English countryside all performed the same function to some extent. They link the familiar with the unfamiliar, the known with the unknown, the world we know with the worlds we cannot know. They are our representatives, our ambassadors, reinforcing the comforting familiarity of existence at the same time as they help us to face the terrifying prospects beyond.

All the characters that appear in such representations are archetypes. They are recognisable by the image they present and we may even know their names, but on a deeper level, an archetype has no name. So the shaman cannot be easily recognised or identified since his most usual face appears as some sort of mask that is larger than life, archetypal. And he is referred to only by his role: as 'the shaman', 'the medicine man' or whatever his people call him.

On a higher level, the shaman – and also to some extent the performer, if he is a good one – is a teacher who presents, communicates and interprets spiritual truths. There has always been a theatrical side to the activities of psychics, seers, augurers and mediums, whether those concerned liked the idea or not. In the same way, nearly all religions work by acting out their messages to their followers. There is nothing wrong with this – it is the only way spiritual truths can be presented when there is no language common to both the physical and the spiritual to bridge the divide.

So both performer and priest, all don some sort of 'official' costume or robe in the carrying out of their office. This is to give them personal anonymity as well as a recognisable image by which they can be identified.

for this new and utterly different lifestyle. I have described elsewhere how on the eve of my first appearance at a Psychic Fair, needing to find a new name I could use on promotional leaflets and with no idea of 'who' I was now intended to be, I sought inspiration from my own books. Recollecting once inventing the perfect pseudonym for the character of a burly lorry driver who wrote tender romances in his spare time, I decided this was possibly as appropriate as I might get in a hurry and my appearance on the psychic scene was consequently made as 'Dawn Rose'. Though I secretly regarded this as a kind of in-joke it became the name by which I worked and was known to everyone throughout my years in London. Friends I made then find it difficult even now to equate their workmate and old pal – or even sitters their psychic consultant 'Dawn' - with Dilys Gater, the writer of books.

The Mask

Traditionally the shaman, as communicator with spirits and other worlds, has to be separated from the person we normally know by some kind of mask, whether donned only occasionally during ceremonies or more or less permanently. The mask provides a no-place, a threshold between. When a mask is in place, one personality and identity is suspended and provision is made for another to be – in its due course – assumed. The mask enables this potentially difficult and dangerous process to be carried out safely and can be put aside when it has been completed. The shaman's mask is of vital relevance: as a maker of journeys between worlds, it is one of the tools, as it were, of his trade.

The world of masks is both ancient and yet very much of today. From the dawn of history masks have been used as a recognised part of living - for protection, for empowerment, for celebration and ritual. Masks of skin, of straw, of fabric or wood, of leather, of plaster, of gold, of feathers or precious or bronze, of bone; animal heads, funeral masks, gladiators' and warriors' masks, devil masks, dragon masks, carnival masks, actors' masks, mummers masks. Ancient shamans used face and body paint, animal skins, tree branches and leaves, to help them connect with spirits of the natural world.

The masked figure can be everything or nothing. Anyone, everyone or no-one. Yet masks are not intended to effect a permanent transformation. They may appear solid and unmoving – indeed that is the usual effect of a mask – but in fact their role is essentially active rather than passive. They work paradoxically, revealing as well as concealing, enabling passage through of what would not be possible otherwise. They allow for the utmost flexibility.

Assume a mask and you make a statement – sometimes a very precise and detailed statement, for masks have always provided the symbolic language traditionally used to keep oral teachings alive. In some cultures, stunning ceremonial masks provide the 'shorthand' enabling the telling of long and complicated stories. The mask itself does not need explanation, working by its own particular kind of 'shorthand' in representation of that people, that tribe or culture.

Masks can immediately and recognisably represent 'who' you are – the image you choose to present to the world - as well as hide the image you desire to conceal. They can also represent 'what' you are (ie: what you choose to represent yourself as) at the same time as they can free you from it. The mask makes a statement but it can also negate a statement or assumption. The mask is not just the physical object, it is what you choose to do with it.

that is actually the truth? Which is the true reality, the everyday or the ceremonial face the shaman or the magician assumes in order to make the connection? Which is the mask?

And which comes first, the mask or the reality it represents? Not every shamanistic culture seems to concern itself with masks. Indeed some books on the subject of shamanism do not mention masks at all. But peoples such as the Intuit Indians of North America – closely connected to the Siberian Tungus tribes from whom the concept of the shaman as we now understand it is thought to have originated – have an intensely rich and detailed tradition of social and ceremonial mask-making and wearing.

When I studied something of the making of masks in American Indian traditions, I found that the art of the mask-maker is not as static as people imagine. The Indians do not just 'put on' a mask, or 'assume' it. Perhaps this is what we like to do for fun at carnival time, where new identities are assumed in order to free the hidden personality to live a different life without constraint. But in many cultures, the person for whom a mask is made – or the one to whom it is passed on later – plays an intensely significant and honourable role as its keeper. He is the honoured, sometimes the chosen one, the one who is worthy to wear and to 'dance the mask.'

Reg Davidson, a Native North American artist and member of the Haida Rainbow Creek Dancers, is quoted in Gary Wyatt's book *Spirit Faces* as confiding that: 'The first Eagle headdress I carved didn't fit on anybody's head. It wasn't until I learned how to dance that I understood the art.'

'Dancing the mask' is a life's work, a continual learning process. For the masks are not just objects behind which identities can be hidden, they are the narratives, the powers, the journeys in themselves. And the dancing of the mask is something that involves great knowledge, wisdom and skill as well as stamina and energy.

So what does this tell the novice about the role of the shaman?

The mask is not in itself the idol or god to be worshipped, though it may be the way to find the deity, the face to recognise, the history and description of everything involved in worshippers and worshiped. It is the flexibility of this kind of image which gives such a different concept to the more usual idea of the mask as a 'cover-up', whether of only the eyes or of the whole face.

A covered-up version fits only the 'I am' who will not change but simply assume different disguises. This kind of person has fossilised into nothing but a stiff outline of his or her self, it is dead before its time, only going through the motions of life.

Why did I never recognise any of the shamans I might have met during the course of my own journeyings? Here we have the answer. For one of the most fascinating aspects of the shaman is that you are never likely to know him from any description because he is never visible. He hides behind not just one mask but many. In the phraseology of some cultures, he can 'shapeshift'. He can be an animal, a bird, anything: 'shapeshifting', changing faces, is a part of his trade. Yet paradoxically it is because he remains always truly himself that this can be achieved.

Dance, Movement, Sound

Tomorrow will be my dancing day,
I would my true love did so chance
To see the legend of my play,
To call my true love to my dance.

Dance, dance, wherever you may be
I am the lord of the dance said he
I lead you on wherever you may be
I lead you all in the dance said he.

These are the words of some of the most ancient of English carols, referring back to hidden and even lost rites and ceremonies. For the shaman has always been a dancer, sometimes a masked dancer, sometimes naked and vulnerable as he offers himself to the beat of the drum-skin and lets his limbs become possessed by the rhythms of forces outside himself.

There is something magical and powerful about the dance, whatever kind of dancing it is. This explains why most religions and cults include ceremonial dances, often with ritual music and instruments, to bind their followers close and to provide a 'gateway' for newcomers to pass through before they commit themselves or are accepted. There are many instances on record of the 'White Man' (because it was the 'White Man' who did most of the exploring and invading) being invited to take part in the dance rituals of primitive tribes as a gesture of friendship.

Music and dance are further tools of the shaman's trade. Through rhythm and dance he can enter other worlds, invoking trance states of altered consciousness that provide a release, freeing him from the confines of his body.

part of group therapy or a means of reaching out to discover and make contact with themselves as well as others - you can see an emergence of the essential pure spirit within, the fineness, generosity and unreserved loving that marks the presence of what human beings of all races recognise as the soul, the spark of the divine, the link with God. This awareness may not last for long beyond the scope of the dance, for the trance-like state of refined and elevated existence is, for most people, almost impossible to retain in day-to-day living.

It was while watching a group of ordinary people performing in a dance presentation at the Mind Body Spirit Festival in London in 1995 that I first realised I was watching something very magical. I had danced myself, studying ballet and tap, flamenco and other sorts; witnessed memorable performances in the past. But this was something very different. For the first time I was aware of reverence, awe, almost fear. I had the sense of standing, as they say, on holy ground.

Or perhaps this time, because I was consciously treading a spiritual path, I was given the eyes to see. Whatever it was, I observed the blossoming of the soul and the resulting ability to reach out of the body to take the hands, as it were, of other souls, whatever their nature. It was one of the most beautiful experiences I have ever encountered and marked a turning point in my awareness of the nature of transcendental experience, particularly that of others.

I had by this time become familiar with my own psychic and spiritual work taking me to many planes of existence, to the higher levels and to recognising and communicating with spirits, entities and angels. On the occasion I have just mentioned earlier, I suddenly appreciated dance as essentially about not performance but communication, about finding a common language and a meeting ground, common ground.

I also realised, with the kind of visionary insight common with many other thinkers and mystics before me, that this world, which is represented to us, the inhabitants of it as solid and permanent, the human condition as the happiest, where humanity can reach out to the stars, is also immeasurably sad; but one in a series of levels, a difficult school where we must learn, sometimes indeed, possibly a vision of hell itself.

Matthew Arnold described it in *Dover Beach* as:

...the world, which seems
To lie before us like a land of dreams,
So various, so beautiful, so new,
Hath really neither joy, nor love, nor light,
Nor certitude, nor peace, nor help for pain:
And we are here as on a darkling plain
Swept with confused alarms of struggle and flight,
Where ignorant armies clash by night.

But is this really the truth, or simply a jaded and cynical vision of only the most obvious aspect of the sadness of the whole cycle of physical life and its capacity for suffering?

We can appreciate now the importance of the shaman as entertainer, even as Fool. It is he who plays a vital role in balancing and complementing the weight of all the pain, darkness and evil inherent in existence.

For the activities of the shaman, like the concept of the medicine wheel, place a limit for us on what is limitless. They give the chaotic and formless unknowable some kind of shape, some sort of perspective. And essentially – though possibly in

'Ah love', said Matthew Arnold, in one same poem, ...
true to one another'. While watching the dancers that
afternoon I felt my own soul expand with the kind of love that
is the answer to all our sufferings and pain: love and
awareness, understanding, compassion and the driving out of
fear.

Dance has always been there, very basic and ancient,
movement and progression in forms such as rounds, patterns,
mazes. Such shapes are intensely meaningful to the shaman
for they reflect the twists and turns, the ups and downs, the
forms and patterns of life and death. They embody the
progressions of the soul on its journey of discovery and the
quest for self-knowledge and wisdom.

Even scientific knowledge recognises the inherent dance of
existence. In quantum physics we find the movement of all
particles in their random restlessness – and in fact all cosmic
activity can be represented as dancing – the patterns of
neurons and protons within the body, fire dancing on the
hearth, even the sun was said by the ancients to dance in the
sky.

One of the most interesting of the tarot cards is the Wheel of
Life, signifying chance, fate, destiny and the random working
out of cosmic unfolding. This concept has been reflected in
sacred rounds and dances of all cultures, the turning of the
wheel fuelled by the energy with which those who
participated performed the dance. Each step we take, however
apparently small, holds meaning and significance, since as
the ancients intuitively knew, all life is intertwined and
related.

The riddles and shapes of dance are everywhere. The ancient Greek source of the word for 'dance', 'orso' meant 'a ritual pattern of dynamic expression'. Megalithic stone circles, the shapes of the Egyptian pyramids and prehistoric burial mounds all reflect the on-going movement of life, death and rebirth. Many times the pattern of the dance was symbolically marked out. On the floor of Chartres Cathedral for instance, there is a pattern of a labyrinth or maze dance, while mazes have been discovered in parts of Scandinavia and throughout the ancient pagan world constructed of stone, the names by which they are referred to reflecting the meaning 'to twist or turn'.

Within the maze, the soul searches for its way, searches to find meaning in the apparently random and meaningless as it follows unclear paths. And within the heart of the labyrinth it must confront the monster that lurks there, the dragon, the Minotaur, flesh-eating projection of its greatest dreads and fears. Within the maze we must seek out and confront the deepest, darkest and most terrifying embodiment of what is within the depths of ourselves. On Crete and in parts of Greece, the tradition associated with the labyrinth was called the Crane Dance (in other places, the association was with the stork), both of these water birds having links with the Goddess and traditionally regarded as bringing good fortune.

But the patterns and dances, as we can see, are not confined to movement but reflected in endless linking threads that reach across the whole spectrum of life. The Scandinavian word for 'maze' signifies 'a state of bewilderment or confusion', related words in Swedish and Norwegian indicating a more languid or dreaming condition. The dancing in maze and spiral forms, like the drumming and sounds which are traditionally associated with the activities of shamans, serve the purpose of creating a state of altered consciousness or trance that is 'between the worlds'. The dancer – the shaman – is thus enabled to travel through the ritual to the point

Native dancers move in accordance with a drumbeat, the drum symbolising the heartbeat of life, the pulse of all living, the basic fundamental rhythm. The drum is also a circle, and in its shape as well as sound represents, as does the pattern of the dance, the circle of eternity. A circle has no end, past, present and future are endless and formless, and the drum sounds the eternal rhythms.

By its quickening or slowing beats, the drum changes the heartbeat of the dancer or the listener, evoking the trance state that will allow the mind to wander into those other realms where enlightenment can be found. Rattles warn off the evil spirits which might otherwise enter into consciousness or find themselves a place to occupy, and it is no accident that shamanic drumming and dancing is often accompanied by repetitive chanting that blots out the awareness of reality. Wild leaping, spinning and whirling further creates 'bewilderment or confusion' in the senses and facilitates a letting go of all conscious awareness and volition.

Changeling Child

Changeling child I was
Snatched by imps
Loosed from my father's kitchen.
My mother was the Morrigan
The power of sexuality and death
I think.

Beneath the visor of knight's challenge
That made men tremble
There was always a woman's body
Supple, boneless, a moppet my father had
created from wax.
I played with lightning bolts in my cradle
Later took on the dark powers
They scarred me but I survived.

It was always dark there
I was unhappy in the light
I feared its power not to harm
But to heal me.

I fear it still
But somewhere there rises a sun
To clothe me in golden splendour
And give me substance.

Nothing to do
But draw each breath, hoping the earth
Will not crack.

DG

A mask infers some kind of false identify, some sort of concealment of the truth. The term 'masquerade' is defined in the dictionary as 'show, false, pretence', even the term 'masque' (meaning a theatrical performance) is something artificial, something contrived. How can we be sure of our identity? Are we the same individuals as we were yesterday? Which part of us, known to different people, is the real one? Which of the voices in which we speak is our true voice, which face we present at different times to the world is our own face?

Parents do not know the person who lives with the lover of their child; the elderly may bemoan the fact that they have outlived their old friends and there is nobody who knows them 'as myself' any more. If you were to meet your self of twenty years ago in the street, would you recognise him or her? Would you want to?

In magic the true name, the true identity, is of immense relevance and importance. Yet like everything else in the universe we are all constantly in a process of change. Not only our appearance changes as we pass through our life, our names – or the names people know us by – change as well. Women marry and take on their husband's name, work-mates know us by nicknames that might be different to the ones our parents or offspring would recognise. Many people lead double or even multiple lives, some of which are not known to the others - and I'm not referring here to cases of 'split personality' or clinical states like schizophrenia, though consideration should perhaps be given to the point where fragmentation of the personality becomes a 'case' in need of attention or help.

In my own case, the search for an identity, for a persona I could feel comfortable with, went on throughout my life. I had appeared under other 'by-lines' besides my own, some male. Publicity photographs on book covers and so on were commented on not because people recognised me from them, but because 'you look so different, I'd never have known it was you!'

I had been vainly trying for years to re-invent myself and discover the 'image' that reflected the true 'me'. My friend Micola, who worked in the world of high fashion and who has always been for me the embodiment of elegance, chic and classy good taste, always brushed aside my worries about my size and failing experiments with the wrong kind of clothes, assuring me generously that I created my own style and that she admired me for it. Yet even though my hair changed colour every few months and my 'style' veered erratically between glittering circus sequins, ethnic patchwork and a mysterious (though bulky) fur-swathed Russian countess effect, the only thing I really seemed to have achieved throughout it all was an increasing awareness of the essential truth we have been discussing in this chapter: that however I tried to make myself different and discover some alternative image, the result, paradoxically, was the exact opposite. Variation and disguise did not hide me. I was never going to be anyone other than myself, even if I could not identify that self.

Is a mask, like a name, the image we choose to present to the world to conceal what we really are? Or is it a title we assume in order to establish claims we want to make? How can this concept of deceiving – masquerading – be applied here? Can we be sure we are what – or who – we claim to be, even who we believe we are? Which – or any, or all - is the real, true image of our self?

The Fool, the Wise Fool is the first card of the Major Arcana in the tarot pack. But it is sometimes also the last card, since the wise fool achieves only the wisdom to know that he knows nothing. The shaman has to be consulted and regarded from each side of the mask, in faith

Reading and meditation

More important than the mask we might assume is the true nature of the source from which enlightenment is obtained. The shaman connects with many sources, but the questing soul will be encouraged and comforted if it can encounter some recognisable image with which to identify. Who or what is the godhead? Brother Gregory, in simple language, made the Source recognisable for me. His words presented me with both a god and a goddess image I could accept, tolerant and compassionate as well as challenging.

The source - teachings of Brother Gregory

1

Your god will be in the image of yourself for only so can you truly know him and recognise him. He walks with you along the road and you will at first think him like yourself, a dusty traveller, his robe frayed, his feet in sandals tired from the journey, his staff lifted more and more weightily.

Towards evening, in the twilight, he will stop, leaning on his staff, and angrily you will say, Have we not reached the inn yet? - you are no better a guide than many another and worse than some. You must do better for me than this. I do not believe you can do all you claimed.

eyes look at you, and you will know yourself to be nothing and less than nothing and this power such that it can take all into itself like so many grains of dust.

Eternities of life and death pass in an eyeblink, and yet you will know within your soul that the tiniest particle of your heart and mind and body, your striving and struggling, your deviations, your boredoms and failures and all the things of which you are ashamed are nothing in the face of the fact that you look into your own eyes and see there what you truly are and if not, then what you can be.

Transformation upon transformation follows the enlightenment, and yet at the end, it was all known at the beginning and it is no different, only the same.

2

Oh my son, you need not another, you have creation itself to bring you the miracles of snowdrop and lily of the valley, the purity and sweetness in a wreath of tiny white stars nodding amid the dewy green leaves. The Maiden, the Queen, the Empress, are the faces of another goddess and for you it is not the shadowed walks beneath the dark trees.

And yet you are young, my son, and reach out to the face misted in the glass, and the eyes that haunt you, and wish a presence to comfort you and lead you into the brilliance of that other world. And she will come and be neither maiden nor queen nor empress and will be created out of your need and your giving so that dimly at first you will see the outline and form in the mirror and then submit in wondering fearfulness to the touch of her fingers.

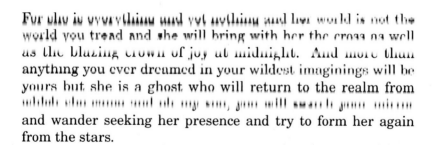

For she is everything and yet anything and her world is not the world you tread and she will bring with her the cross as well as the blazing crown of joy at midnight. And more than anything you ever dreamed in your wildest imaginings will be yours but she is a ghost who will return to the realm from which she comes and she may slip, you will search your mind and wander seeking her presence and try to form her again from the stars.

Within the deepest water and the barest peak where the brown brushwood burned by the summer touches the coppery of the sun and dull gleam of the sky you will lay down your sword and offer yourself to the goddess who arches across the universe day to day, morn to evening and you will find her the power to transform and transfigure to initiate you to knighthood in the mysteries.

It must happen to each in their own way my dear son. It was not for me and I never sought it but you have been chosen for that very reason and purpose, and I will remain with my cloisters and sage and fennel and leave you to climb the path to that tormented peak and the dark and bitter sun and the powers which devour and the struggles and confused clashes with the dark.

For me the madonna was enough, serene and unmoving, but my dear son I have known the devils and familiars of the witch – but not this, not the lost hells for her. But if this is your destiny my dear son then go and find her for she is powerful and fearsome and her consort must be so and of equal power, and equally must pass through the dark.

If you can look into her face and live then you will find whatever you wish my dear son, and you will have earned whatever is your heart's desire.

and the major benefits will continue only as long as you continue to practice.

Chuck Jones
Make Your Voice Heard; An Actor's Guide to Increased Dramatic Range Through Vocal Training

The city has its own gifts to offer, one of which is the enormous range of opportunities to experience different dramatic presentations and theatre as well as classes, courses and study groups. The aspiring shaman will probably not need, for example, to perform imitative animal dances in order to petition the natural world for a successful hunt, but he can connect and attune with the pulse of the natural world in ways which might not at first be apparent.

1 Watch a performance or study a Shakespeare play where one of the characters is a Fool (eg. *King Lear*, *Twelfth Night*)

2 Consider the function of popular TV 'soaps' in relation to the presentation of archetypal figures who help us make sense of the human situation.

3 Enrol for a dance, mime or movement course; take a class or workshop in circus skills; investigate Greek drama.

4 Go clubbing, listen to rap music, jazz, drums, feel the pulse of the city. To the urban dweller these sounds are just as relevant as native ceremonial chants and ceremonies, perhaps more since they form the natural background to everyday living.

and hear youth's heavy feet
stomping sunshine into the earth.

once, I was a flower.

PG

Chapter 5

In the Flames of the Fire

It is difficult for others to appreciate that someone who loves the city may be 'spiritual' and in tune with the natural world, without necessarily longing to rush to the open spaces of the countryside at every opportunity. One of the most important lessons for any questing soul to learn is to be true to itself, however this may seem to be taking it in the wrong direction. A common misconception is that there is no meeting ground between urban and rural, that you have to hate the city if you are a country-lover, and vice versa.

While venturing into the wilderness, the shaman of some indigenous tribe would have rested, gathered strength by his fire. The element of fire signifies many things –cleansing, purification, regeneration. In the flames of the fire come the images, the visions that open the channels to enlightenment. But the campfire of the traveller, that warning and comforting fire protecting against the shapes lurking in the dark beyond, reassuring the seeker of safety and rest, is not the only kind of fire where such inspiration may be found today. The city dweller need not feel excluded from elemental visions.

Any urban landscape is in a constant state of renewal, whether rebuilding after disasters of war and tragedy, or simply expanding hopefully in new directions. Fires crackle clearing the rubbish on demolition sites, fires warm the night watchmen, fires cheer the homeless, the drop-outs, the lost and the left behind in our busy, bustling metropoli. Anyone

Though the urban sprawl creeps ever onwards, absorbing into itself former green spaces so that many regard this as the ultimate tragedy, it has to be placed into a wider context. At one time all spaces were green spaces, thick forest, the haunt only of wild beasts. Man's aspiring is what has created cities in the first place, and the shamanic vision comprehends that what is given and accepted has to be in some way paid for. Nothing is achieved without some sacrifice, some pain, some loss.

Speaking personally, though I loved London and found spiritual enlightenment in the city, this did not mean I was unable to appreciate the gifts of nature and connect with them in a country setting. The world in which I grew up, the wild Welsh countryside celebrated in *Celtic Wise Woman* will be part of my brain and bone until I die. One's spiritual roots might indeed lie far from the hustle of the city – but there is no obligation to live continually in that place. I do not need to travel physically into Wales every time I need its particular solace and inspiration. And when I do go back, as with renewing old and loved friendships, the rarer such encounters, the more meaningful they can become.

The lines below were written in my twenties, long before I was aware of any consciously spiritual questing, far less psychic vocation. They were broadcast as part of a fifteen-minute 'play of voices' celebrating my own particular background and heritage that I called *Welsh Tapestry*.

A Celtic Identity

I

Red is the faded parchment of her history,
Tattered and bloody, yet proudly worded
And stirring to the pulse when the bard sings in the firelight.

Sing on, blind harper, I hear and my heart quickens.
Sing, and the ghosts of your torchlit audience stir in the dim past.
We two are linked in blood
I and that shadowy being you knew, and I can but sense.

A cup-bearer? A vassal? A slave?
Perhaps, but he would have held his head as nobly as his master;
His shoulders were as broad, his eyes as fiercely blue,
And this land took his blood as proudly as the blood of princes.

He too was of the dragon –
The dragon that lies across the valley,
Half-tamed now, but still crouched warily.
And those who do not know might think him
A ridge of moors, dark and still marked with scattered snow,
Though it is Spring, and the daffodils are out.

100

The Hall – grey stone, a ...
Symmetry and precision dreamed
By the keen mind of Inigo Jones.

Its walls held the dignity of the centuries,
Its sightless windows constantly overlooked
The muted tapestry of the Welsh hills.
It had its place in history's panorama too –
Legends, a blood-stained room, a ghost.

But should I climb the wall – that still stands – and I no
longer a child,
Would I find the past again?
My foot would grope falteringly for floors no longer there,
My senses shrink from the dark well of the fallen stairs.

So with the cottage that stood in the hollow – there I am a
ghost already,
Wearily seeking its roses, scarlet and white,
Its lilac and its blossoming apple tree.
In my memory the path beckons, sun-dappled,
Potent and heady with mingled fragrances.

But no wall for me to climb to reach it, only the twisted thorn-
hedge of the years.
What lies behind the barrier, there, where the leaves of my
childhood still are green?

Shadows with sunlight in their faces. Like the fragrant echoes
of the roses
Spring from the deep soil of Wales.
Music of the bards in their voices,
Their heritage the blue of proud banners in their eyes.

But there is no path down into the hollow
Where the black cat suns herself against the mellowed wall
Behind the barrier of time there is only
Grass, blowing in the wind, over their quiet graves

Town and Country - No Contest

Many writers before me have admitted to an appreciation of
the inspirational – even spiritual - qualities of the urban
scene, though they might well have possessed undeniable and
celebrated links with the natural world of the countryside.
William Wordsworth's *Ode on the Intimations of Immortality*
is perhaps one of the best known expressions of shamanic
vision in Western literature, but he also wrote the following
sonnet, which speaks for itself about his feelings for London.

Upon Westminster Bridge
Sept. 3, 1802

> Earth has not anything to show more fair:
> Dull would he be of soul who could pass by
> A sight so touching in its majesty:
> This City now doth like a garment wear

Never did sun more beautifully steep
In his first splendour valley, rock, or hill;
Ne'er saw I, never felt a calm so deep!

The river glideth at his own sweet will:
Dear God! the very houses seem asleep;
And all that mighty heart is lying still!

And this was my own more humble offering in urban appreciation, written about the same time as my Celtic verses. Long
before I lived in London I spent nearly ten years in this
beautiful and historic English city on the borders of Wales.

Chester

River-girded city, wrapped in the dark robe of its history
Lies, broken castle towers between the water-lilies,
Coruscates softly, dim green imagery.
And, no Lady of Shallot, I am free
To look out of my high window.
My mirror does not crack from side to side,
But treasures secrets, faces, forms
Enough to ransom me in coins of love.

No minstrels bring lutes to midnight serenade,
Or twine with my priceless pearls of moonlight, gold;
No slaves bear rare and secret-scented flowers:
Yet brightly dazzles this oriental splendour,
Scheherazade, ringed by my colonnades,
Watch nightly, caravans through the western gates,
And seek the rose that heralds the eastern morning.

Going Within: Guardians, Guides and Teachers

Love Child

In silver hands,
He cupped a crescent moon,
Flight-feather of the
Hovering canticle-bird.

Aeons later,
Love-child's brother
Searches purple
Charge-lands
And far-out nebulae –
Through telescopes
Of wish-bone thought.

PG

If prophecy be the liberation of the diviner parts of the soul, in truth the cause is no other than illumination emanating from the very gods themselves and spirits coming forth from them
Lamblichus

...the core of shamanic practice is a lot of time spent alone. It looks like alone, but in fact it is not quite alone because there are all kinds of realities going on that you are examining
Malidoma Patrice Some

105

I was with you when you came into the world, I came too for as
I was able along the way and held you before you went from us
to represent us in your body. It was difficult to let you go,
knowing your way would be hard and lonely, but we have been
with you throughout all, if you could have seen us

Mist

It was only when I considered the nature of shamanic
experience in more depth that I began to understand the true
relationship between the shaman and his inspirational
Otherworlds, including the world of animals. Though brought
up in a country environment with cats and dogs in the home, I
have admitted I never felt particularly drawn to the
farmyard, the stables, the small-holding, the wild in its
rawest and least sentimental aspects. Many city people, even
if they are doting and devoted pet owners, probably feel the
same. Does this mean that if you live in an urban
environment there can be no sense of true shamanic
connection with the natural world?

The term 'anima' signifies the soul: 'animal worlds' are
Otherworlds where spirits of the earth, animals, plants and
other natural things may be confronted on their own ground,
and in order to gain access to these dimensions we have seen
that the shaman enters the trance state, leaving his physical
self behind as he travels into realms where the gods/the dead/
animals or other beings may be contacted. It is in this way
that he makes his journeys into Otherworlds and also returns.
It made far more sense to me to realise that it is not necessary
for the shaman to go anywhere physically: the other realms
are not physical planes - even the 'animal world' of shamanic
connection is within rather than without.

In trance, where the personality and will are suspended, the
body is open to possession or invasion by, or even union with,
other entities. It is these entities – whether perceived as the
god or some other spirit – which by speaking through the

Crowning achievement of the trance state, according to all religions, is complete possession by or union with the deity - in this respect prayer is another method of inducing trance that invites divine participation, though the more recognisable 'shamanic' methods are through chanting, drumming or frenzied movement.

The extreme experience of mysticism as expressed in the mystical trance is, according to all who have ever achieved it, of such intense glory that all other experience pales into nothing by comparison. The life of the mystic becomes filled with joy, meaning and a sense of completion, oneness with the source and font of all life. Reality is transcended and the mystic sees his whole existence in relation to everything else and becomes aware of the essential truths, the great mysteries. More significantly, all answers to all questions are given, known and understood – at least for the duration of the experience.

During his mental journeyings the shaman will glimpse this state often as he encounters and works with guides who advise and teach him, though he might not necessarily regard the guides themselves as divine but as forming aspects, fragments of the divinity. The guides, guardians and teachers who present themselves, usually initially during the vision quest or traumatic incidents that mark the shamanic vocation, may be perceived as ancestors, animals, birds or other sources of power and wisdom. They can include be called 'Spirit Guides' (sometimes perceived, as we have seen, as relatives or other spirits of the dead), since shamans are mediums who can communicate with the departed as well as with beings who inhabit other realms.

wandered accidentally, or were summoned without realising it, into other worlds. In English tradition, it was the Queen of Elfland who bestowed a 'tongue that could not lie' on Thomas the Rhymer, poetic prophet of the 13th century. The gift came in the form of 'an aipple frae a tree' – linking prophetic or divinatory powers with the fruit from the tree of knowledge eaten by Adam and Eve in the Garden of Eden. It is no coincidence that the apple is connected in magical lore with foresightedness and all kinds of esoteric mysteries. The apple tree was sacred to the Celts, referred to as the Silver Bough.

The practice of working with and obtaining information from the spirits of the dead, called necromancy, has long been regarded with fear and suspicion, since the necromancer is considered to violate the natural laws when communicating with those who are beyond physical contact - in some cases, for instance in forms of voodoo, the actual corpses of the dead can be involved. Adepts of the blacker arts have always been unhealthily drawn to dead bodies and the prospect of reanimating them as sources of power, though enlightened traditions recognise the body as simply the shell left when the spirit or soul has departed; it is enough merely to connect with the souls or essences of the dead on a spiritual level.

The shaman is, more than any other kind of visionary or seer, in close contact with the natural world. His inspiration, his wisdom, is intimately connected and intertwined with the intuitive, instinctive wisdom of beings other than human, which do not speak with a human voice: it is one of his functions to give expression to such wisdom, to absorb and diffuse it, to allow it to become manifest through him.

The guides and teachers, advisers and protectors he will encounter are not simply outside influences. Living and working with souls and spirits, whether of humans or other beings, he not only becomes able to tread their various realms with familiarity and confidence, he absorbs those realms, internalising them so that he embodies them and their qualities: the essential is that they are invited within and become one with him, empowering him, whether temporarily or permanently, with their own essential strength and nature.

The shaman lays aside his human realities in order to connect with those other, wider realities and enable them to reveal themselves. This is not easy, and trying to express such concepts in words can sometimes appear to trivialise both the shaman and his utterances. I once wrote, when describing how 'messages' came through to me from other sources, of the practicalities of such a procedure. 'Often the communicating entity cannot convey its thought because it does not communicate in thoughts, far less in words. For me to try and put a sentence together to convey the meaning is rather like having to translate from a caveman who can only grunt, or a bolt of lightning. Suitable words and phrases within my own mind are therefore made use of, and I am aware of this.'

Shamanic guides are all-encompassing, diffusing throughout the personality. Before I came to know Mist, two tiny silvery spirits I called 'Stalk' and 'Blue' had presented themselves to me. I assumed they were my 'Spirit Guides' but later, when I asked Mist who they were, I was given the answer 'they are parts of me'. Very much the same sense came also from other sources, particularly regression sessions I conducted where animal, or even spirit existence, was involved – I received an intense awareness of a corporate whole, a oneness where all parts reflect and support the rest.

Yet the voices that inspire the shaman are also his own voice, hard-won enlightenment revealing only what has always been dancing sessions, and at various stages carried out the traditional kind of shamanic journeys to 'meet' my power animals (discussed in *Celtic Wise Woman*, which provides meditational guidelines on how to do this yourself) where I discovered my particular 'totems' to be the stormy petrel and also the wren – both, interestingly enough, birds. But the essential understanding came in a more subtle form.

It is not for the shaman to 'know it all'. Often he knows less as he progresses. The best illustrations I can give personally are from my own notes, written as I worked with my guides. From the following three examples you will see that the questioning and progression very much outweighs the sense of knowing. I found as often happened in my own mind-working, meditating with guides and spirits, that it was difficult sometimes to differentiate between what I was trying to say or think myself and what my guides were saying to me. The voices, whether within or without, had become one.

Stalk and Blue (Two tiny silvery presences, like small sparks of light)

'Stalk and Blue – looking back to you, I see big footprints across the rooftops, silver as rain on grey slates. How can they be so big if you are so small? Is this the link or just the sadness of this world?

'I am not sad, yet this world pulls me down. Why should we have to plan in advance, fill up time? Why must we have Time? And past time, too? Maybe on those days it was not raining, what I see was frost or grey light. Or shadows? The effort to lift the spirit was great. Yet you are shining now – I see the silver hound, the signpost – what else at this moment? 'Simplistic big basket with a card, full of bluebells, pussy willow, forget the hill, just being Richly 'The roofs don't matter. The they really empty?'

'In my end is my beginning – but what if the end came first and we are working backwards, perhaps unravelling all the bad and bad things – bringing blue sky and yellow light to the slate roots, even pulling down the roofs and making space and light? Going back to space and light ourselves?'

Mist

Mist my love, my darling, all around is noise and heaviness and I simply hold the threads together – apparently. Tell me something love to help as it is difficult.

- snow whirling, shining white and sparkling and in the midst I am, you are, we are, we will be and have been –

Oh my love keep close as it is so lonely and I am so tired. Only you and myself are real. The rest is something I have to leave behind.

You put the book (*Celtic Wise Woman*, on which I was then working) into my mind. Yes, I have tasks to do, and this is one, so that my difficulties are taken care of in the future. The book I can do and it will be good – you have given me the insight and the ability. I can do it and do it well.

What about Ireland my darling? (I was wondering whether I should try and make the trip) Give me some guidance – if I feel well enough I would like to go. A place where I can go? Does that matter? Or does it not? Here are the problems and yet when you are here I am fulfiled and not alone. And you lift the burdens my love, bring the light back and the shine of sun on snow and the silent communication.

- waterfall glistening, the snow fluttering and cold keen air and also the sun, even though it is winter. And I am not alone.

Mist my love, my darling, thank you for my self.

to be perpetrated on this body, which is already be—
the spirit is like a lamp within – and will bring the shell
safely through the deep water and batterings, refine the body
to allow the spirit peace and quiet, calm of soul and mind. It
will protect you, and ease the scars so that they fade. Hold on
to the spirit and let the dark pass. You can do this, gently. Be
patient. You will come through and over, rather than against
the flow. Just be, accept, reach out to the light.

Animals have always been close to humans and important to
them, many religions teaching metampsychosis, the
transmigration of souls, even incorporating life as plants or
stones. My book *Understanding Past Live*, was written after I
had been working for some years as a psychic and included
accounts of seventy cases of regression to past lives I had
personally dealt with. One of the chapters was about past
lives as animals, for I found while conducting regressions that
some people did indeed seem to have lived previously as
animals. I wanted to pursue this subject in a further book -
which actually never appeared, since the publisher was
uncomfortable about the way my research was heading - it's
proposed 'blurb' explaining that: 'She became so intrigued ...
she decided to investigate the whole concept of past lives as
animals – and indeed the significance and meaning of animals
themselves – in depth.

'Applying her journalistic training to carry out her
investigation open-mindedly and without sentimentality, she
records accounts of animal regressions – often to previous
human beings – and startling new evidence to suggest that
animals may actually be a superior, rather than an inferior,
form of life than human beings. All those who love animals
and are inspired by them will find this book validates the fact

that animals are not only our friends, they may be our Guardian Angels', spiritual guides and helpers as well as being closely related to us in indeed, our other, or higher selves as well'

When I 'regressed' my own little pet dove Glory, I noted a sense of connection to 'a vague swirl of silver – a corporate soul, innocence and purity – part of a richer and more complex spiritual energy. Spark of god, being, the life force - .' I came across almost these same words recently in an article by John Starkey, who heals and works with animals, communicating directly with them Writing in *Psychic News*, he declared: 'I believe they (animals) are in touch with 'Pure Spirit' and therefore have not been influenced by human-type logic and all its restrictions. Consequently, I am always wary of humans who are not kind to animals.'

But far beyond simply being kind, or even being able to pick up what animals are saying, or connect with them psychically as I have done in past life regressions, the shaman's connection with the animal world – the roles animals play – provides a far richer and more complex picture immensely significant in deepening our understanding.

Most religions teach that the life force, 'the god', is within every existing thing and that everything is therefore related and possesses a spirit. But though we may accept this wider view – even incorporating the concepts touched on above - and try to follow its shamanic principles, we are inclined to anthropomorphise animals and even insects, plants, stones and inanimate objects because that is how our human brains work. We generally regard them as essentially like ourselves, only different – 'our furred and feathered friends'. We also do this with concepts of 'Spirit Guides' and other-world teachers, angelic or higher beings - even to some extent the deity itself.

114

animal and natural kingdoms have been affected by his influence to some degree. But the shaman's experience of the natural world is very different. It is bloody, ruthless, unpitying, teaching him to view realities as they are without flinching: it reveals the dark and dreadful side of existence as well as the bits that will fit within comfortable boundaries.

This wider vision assists us as we attempt to view the unviewable. It helps us to accept the apparently unthinkable and unbearable in suffering and pain, the natural world's seeming callousness in its disregard for the weak and selection of the fittest.

Cases of past lives where animal existences appeared seemed to me to give clear teaching on this difficult subject. I encountered among others, a caged gorilla with ancient, sad eyes which was being displayed in a public square in Spain, several hunted bears, and a deer in the moment when it was being torn apart by hounds. These were traumatically terrible experiences that nevertheless brought with them a transcending sense of existing unquestioningly, in pure acceptance, pure trust and faith. I concluded that at least some animal lives might have the function of giving the questing spirit a respite from the tortuous configurations of human striving. An animal, however hard its existence, appears to experience a peace of mind impossible for the human brain to achieve, with worry and anticipatory fear of the future lifted; my experience was of a going back to the pure love and trust which is a direct connection with God. More than that, because animals are in their simplicity wiser than humans, we are through them able to accept the whole of existence – including suffering – so that it becomes transmuted into something else altogether.

The Sacrifice

No achievement is easy, all learning and progression involves struggle, often seemingly unbearably so. The shaman's vision recognises the necessity of suffering in order to achieve the enlightenment bestowed, the necessity of sacrifice. There is, however, one significant distinction. Sacrifice has to be carried out willingly, it is not forced but must be freely accepted, even offered or sought after. In ancient shamanic cultures the youths and maidens – or those of any age – chosen to be sacrificed were highly regarded; because they were to make a blood sacrifice on behalf of the rest they were honoured, sometimes as though they were touched with the divine themselves. Civilisations like those of the Aztecs and the Mayans understood the significance of such sacrifices, however brutal, accepting them as part of the need of everyday existence.

This same tradition can be found in Native North American culture. The Plains Indians performed the Sun Dance, where they attached hooks through their flesh and endured the agony for as long as they could, in order to seek vision. It is reported that the Sioux Chief Sitting Bull (who was a Huncpapa medicine man) 'danced with his eyes fixed on the sun for 18 hours until he fell unconscious'; at length a great vision came (of victory for the red men). His adopted brother Jumping Bull, 'cut 100 pieces of flesh from his arms with an awl and a sharp knife' in order to achieve his enlightenment.

This concept is difficult for the western mind to understand and there are aspects which seem contradictory. In the American Indian culture, for instance, prisoners were captured for the purpose of, among other things, sacrificial torture. Did they undergo it willingly, did they consent to the agonies they endured? I wondered about that; but the inference was presumably that by allowing themselves to be captured, they had in effect consented to whatever was meted heads. Cannibalism has also been practised for this reason. But these are not aspects the sentimental (or even the 'weekend shaman') like to consider since they go far beyond the superficial to the deepest symbolism, the essential hidden core and mystery of shamanic understanding.

On an atavistic and archetypal level the shaman represents his people, standing as a bulwark between them and the terrible realities they cannot face. Because of who he is he will always be to some degree isolated; never an altogether popular figure, never truly approachable or easy to understand, never a social animal, one of the boys. The shaman in some ways has to assume the role of the Judas goat or the sacrificial creature that is symbolically offered as a token to the gods, he must be willing to live his life to that end. Animals carry out this role all the time; by its very nature it is something that is accepted passively, permitted to happen rather than actively sought or performed. It can be done – and often is – is innocence and in ignorance, explaining how the role of the shaman is instinctive rather than academic. He does not need 'educating', teaching or informing in the generally accepted manner – indeed, this is not possible - but he learns by intuition from his experience, absorbing and embodying the vision.

The function of the sacrifice is to absolve, to carry burdens when no-one else is there to carry them. The shamanic vision sees this wider picture and accepts its inevitability. In making the connection with nature he accepts and links with everything else in whichever way he must, silently acknowledging acquiescence, a willingness to participate, to unquestioningly take whatever is laid upon him.

It is commonly not appreciated that the tree of knowledge encompassed knowledge of both good and evil. And this is why the shaman must tread realms that are difficult, often painful or distressing, and accept truths others find too challenging, too apparently unacceptable, to face. The clear sight of sacrificial victims enables them to see – and to help others to see – the dark side of themselves without flinching, to incorporate it into the whole in order to make human existence bearable. It is only by recognising that we are flawed that we can live with our flaws, frailty and weakness; by accepting that we are unlikeable that we become enabled to like ourselves and consequently others. The victims are empowered through their unique experience to validate the necessary existence of negatives, of cruelty and violence; assisting in comprehension of why people might offend – might even murder - helping those who do to come to terms with themselves without being overcome by shame and despair, by self-loathing, horror and disgust. Simply by treading the difficult worlds of the lost, the damned, the unforgivable as well as the unforgiving, the shamanic victim is empowering the souls that dwell there to emerge into the light.

Though often more instinctively than rationally appreciated, a shaman is like a confessor. He is able to hear and to see the worst that can be offered to him without blaming or judging. Those functions have to be relinquished. He has no rights, no privileges, no opinions beyond what his vision bestows and his own mental struggle, his own physical pain, has to be given voluntarily, freely endured as an offering to the universe.

His mane with silver mercury threaded fine,
Once rusted coat de-blooded to pewter sheen,
Shattered hindquarters micro-surgically joined,
Befitting the trot between the gates of heaven,
To prance, Pegasus-like, down pearly streets,
He hears, with dulled and fading ache,
The far-off rumble of a distant storm,
Senses, unseeing, the yellow sulphurous fork
Crash through the dumb limbs of a weeping tree,
And, knowing no better, faithful, quiveringly,
To the call to arms,
Lifts up a phantom head and paws the stars.

DG

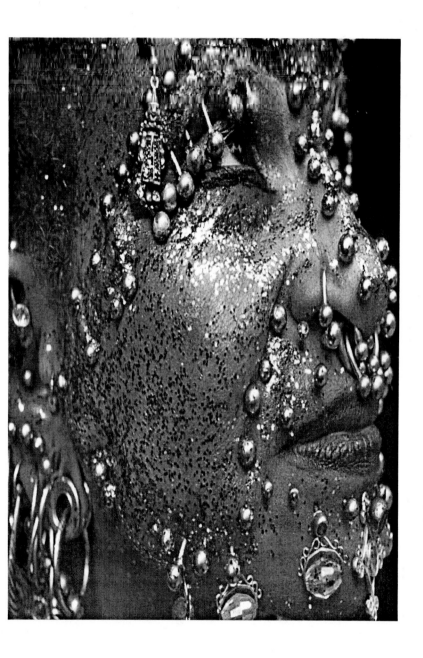

I who am the beauty of the green earth,
And the white moon among the stars,
And the mystery of the waters
Call unto your soul; Arise and come unto me.

I am the soul of nature which gives life to the universe;
From me all things proceed and unto me all things must
return.
And before my face, beloved of gods and men,
Your inmost divine self shall be unfolded
In the rapture of the infinite.

And you who think to seek for me,
Know your seeking and yearning will avail you nothing
Unless you know the mystery –
That if that which you seek you do not find within yourself
You will never find it without.
For behold: I have been with you from the beginning and
I am that which is attained at the end of desire.

From the Celtic tradition
Author unknown

Native shamanic peoples believe all life is sacred, that all are there for each other and there is a recognised role for each - but there is no reason why city dwellers cannot sincerely share this vision.

It is often assumed that in order to respect animals - to respect the planet, even - human beings must adopt such a reverential attitude that they deny themselves the necessities of their own evolutionary survival. There must be no killing, no eating meat or wearing fur for instance. But essentially, in the end these have to be personal choices, dictated by each individual's conscience.

The shamanic vision is clear and unclouded by sentimentality; it is the shaman's function to uphold the natural balance, and to interfere with the cycles and rhythms of existence. These, inevitably, must include death as well as life, in order that all species may flourish in their own way. Animals kill in order to eat; this must respected and the killing carried out as efficiently and humanely as possible.

It is true that in Native North American teachings the 'two-leggeds' (human beings) have a duty to care for, conserve and respect the earth. But equally, the 'four-leggeds' (animals) are also believed to intuitively recognise the part they must play. As Larry J. Zimmerman expresses it in *Native North America*, ' Many...(animals) willingly sacrifice themselves to feed and clothe the people.'

Such a mutual respect was an integral part of everyday life. The Plains Indians honoured the buffalo as a source of life-giving sacrifice, and before the great buffalo hunts important ceremonies were held to obtain the consent of the animals to be hunted and killed. Jon E. Lewis tells us in his book *The West* that 'Since Indians believed that the buffalo, like every animal, was an other-than-human person, the beast had to give its consent to die. This was obtained by prayer and reverence. Intricate ceremonials preceded the kill'.

The buffalo were respected by the tribes, their right to life as well as death sacred. It was the white man who instituted killing them for pleasure when there was no necessity for food. Again, decisions of this kind have to be a personal choice.

...e in areas where pain — even death — is transcended and becomes something positive rather than negative, constructive rather than destructive.

I find an expression of this concept in Richard Erdoes' quote of the Medicine Man's chant while setting up a buffalo altar:

Let us honour the bones
of those who gave their
flesh to keep us alive.

Reading and meditation

The offering — words of the goddess

1 *The Maiden*

Beneath the arched branches of the willow, in the deepest shadow, the maiden lies in sacrifice. Her hands and her feet are bound and her hair dips with the willow branches into the water. Green leaves will mirror her eyes as the spirit of the earth possesses her and fills her; the sounds of the water will drown the gasps of her violated mouth.

For ever it must be so, for ever the maiden must wait in bondage for the spirit to come to her and overshadow her. For ever the water must drown the cries of the virgin and the leaves tremble as the trembling of her body when she is again alone.

The heart of the earth beats fierce and strong, stopping the ears of the virgin. She cannot hide for all ways lead to the shadow of the green tree and the murmuring of the water. Bind therefore her hands, spread her hair and let her wait for the earth to come to take her for itself.

To the goddess turn the lost, the bruised and trembling bodies, the bleeding mouths and violated minds. The goddess is all things to all men. She will bind up the scars and gently soothe the pain of memory, so that once again the leaves are green and not crimson, and once more the water sings and does not weep. Lay your pain at the feet of the goddess and she will gladden your heart and lift your soul. Within her glade bloom roses even through the snow, and the nightingale sweetly calls with each rising moon. She brings joy to those who despair and strength to the weak, and illuminates the dark corners of the soul with brightness.

the lions who roam ~~~~~~ ~~~~~
through pain can the soul come to know ~~~~~~ ~~
suffering. Only those who have drunk the poisonous dregs
may sip the sweet waters of harmony and calm.

Draw near, all who would approach the goddess, and do not
cease in your wailing and your torment, for those who have no
needs cannot plead at her altar. In her wisdom and her
goodness, she will lean forward to touch you with the starry
fingers of her right hand. Her touch will remain with you for
ever, and the star sign will be branded upon your forehead, to
mark you as long as you live for one of her own.

3 *The Promise*
Dark is the blood in the cup that will be held to the lips of
those who seek the goddess. Sharp is the knife that will be
held to the throat of those who offer themselves in sacrifice to
her beauty and her power. She will take them like lambs
which cry piteously for their mothers as their little bodies are
seized by the slaughterers. On the hills where those small
bodies so joyously skipped, run the black cloud shadows, and
the ewes mourn with sad eyes. In the abattoir hang the
carcasses, dripping.

Bleak is the path and piercing the thorns which will tear the
feet of the seeker after the goddess. Far is the tower, and even
further the face of the maiden whose loveliness inspired this
quest. The goddess is merciless, and like a falcon she swoops
upon her prey; like the prized Greenland falcon, bird of kings
and princes of royal blood, she drops like a stone to sink her
claws into the flesh of the small creature that cowers below
her.

Yet as the seeker kneels in the early dawn *being* *weeping* at his *window* *and* his *inability*, the goddess will come with the *sweetness* of the pale light, like petals of primrose and *pearl* overlaying the *blue* of the *morning* sky, and her touch will be as the dew falling on his forehead, and her breath will smell of wild blossom, and the purity and the passion of her will drive him down on his knees in adoration.

And he will never more be free of that moment and that glimpse of her face and her form; he will be seized with madness so that the maiden will languish in her tower and only the high path where the snakes curl and the lions roam will exist for him.

The Novice

It was necessary for you to learn in silence, you have been dumb as the beasts and could not but endure, unable to grunt or howl your pain. The patterns of the universe do not speak, they have other words in the moving and the shining, and you have in your silence spoken for many who were unable. The very stones, the lost and dying small things that wander among the dank remainders of an autumn's leaves, the hopeless, all these did you, of light, take in your hands and nurture of your depths of compassion, in silence and in the exile that bound you to a barren and arid plane of which you did not belong.

But within you the sun-shining did not die though it seemed so. You are one of us and with a breath you could wreak more havoc than Krakatoa, save that we do not speak of such things for it is beneath our doing.

You are in our care and beneath the hand of Aescepholus himself. You even as the sun wish to know your way from moment to moment, so does your strength grow as it does with him. But you are in the shadow of the moon, it is

inviolate of all things, who have carried many tiny down
us. Without you the weak would not survive. We honour you,
rest and let us mend your wounds. Let the moonlight be cool,
for when the morning comes you will again blaze in fiery
splendour and mortals stand amazed.

Practical

1 Whether in country or city, it is important to learn to be
still, to accept, to observe, to be part of what is going on and
yet detach yourself - I got used to doing this instinctively over
thirty years as a professional writer. Sit on a park bench, on a
bus, in a café, letting the ebb and flow of life go on around
you, noticing every smallest detail and yet letting it all pass
through. Try to avoid emotional responses, do not become
involved on a personal level. In this way you allow a greater
sense of awareness to develop.

2 Explore the ways in which your own guides may
communicate with you. Apart from the disciplines that have
already been mentioned, try writing down the thoughts that
just come into your head, 'make up' poetry, begin to train
yourself in inspirational writing or 'channelling'. You will
almost certainly find that as a result of practising this kind of
awareness, your artistic gifts of whatever sort – whether for
painting, music or writing – will increase, or if you did not
think you had any, will make themselves apparent. You will
become enabled to view the world around you in a richer,
more subtle way, both relating to it and allowing others to
relate to your vision.

3 Consider the words of *The Offering* and the Monument in this chapter on the nature of suffering, applying them to your own experiences and that of others.

4 Visit museums to study ancient artifacts reflecting the sacrificial ceremonies of ancient/other cultures; look up the writings about such cultures.

now invaders tear inroads
into silence,
muffling cries from a green woodpecker
high on an opulent god-head,
lopped by the greeding blasphemy of axe play.

paws below ground
scratch a frantic earth
for safer depths,
while dry saplings snap.

souls, bark-capped,
flesh-capped, declaim
as bodies, limbs and unborn leaves
crash to a mounting plethora
of wounds that shout for oil and wine,

clenched fist of mass defiance
shakes – but waivers to
the searing rasp of power-saws,
                    and savage muscle

- dwarfed
against the stirring wrath
of a headless, wild Jehovah,
woken.

PG

URban Empowerment:
Getting Equipped

'Winter and thick snow out in the Wilderness,
You are a Wise Woman, and you are kneeling down picking
berries,
You've got a staff, you're wearing purple,
Your hair hangs below your waist.'

Amelia Summerfield,
a Reiki healer, who while carrying out a Reiki healing session
for me, 'saw' me as I had been in a past life.

The city-dweller may appear to have little in common with native shamans. We do not need to don masks and perform ceremonial enactment of tribal history, undertake rain dances or ritually celebrate the return of the sun – popular TV anthropologists and weather forecasters do it for us. So is there actually any point in trying to learn about native mask-making skills, the dancing and drumming and ceremonials of ancient tribes? What relevance do these have to today's urban dweller?

Look around you. A bewildering depth of living, richness, colour and symbolism can be found on all sides in every town or city. And is there, after all, very much difference between the revered robes and masks of shamans of native tribes with their colour and panoply, and the modern forms of disguise and masquerade encountered in buzzing fashion shows? Or between the face paints of the medicine man and the creation of 'other' faces and images in places like the Make-up Department of Selfridges, where I personally have spent many happy hours being treated to 'makeovers' by zealous saleswomen anxious to interest me in their particular brands of power and paint?

Consider the everyday experience of the urbanite as he walks down any High Street or shopping mall: he is subjected to explosions of colour, shape and texture. Paints, blushers, shimmers-sticks, highlighters, smudgers and every kind of ritual adornment for the face and body, sun-specs, fashion hats, jewellery, hair-pieces, tan and bronzing lotions as well as the insidious promise of miracle products that can lift our faces, reduce or reshape our bodies - all these offer the 'good medicine' that was once the prerogative only of the initiate. And why stop at accessories, creams and lotions? Personal programmes are now available to completely make us over so we become other people, more glamorous, more charismatic, far more likely to get what we want out of life. Even the trend in entertainment for 'nobodies' presented with overnight stardom (whether as performers who can actually perform or just as media-hyped 'personalities') offer promises all around us of, if we try hard enough, being able to assume and actually enter in to a whole complete new identity, a whole new assumption of power.

Shamanic masks, the stereotypes of tradition, the costumes and disguises that are used to assist rites of passage and invoke beings beyond ourselves to reveal themselves to us, are surely only formal archetypes, recognisable examples of the masks of everyday living. We intuitively know their significance, magically invoking their power all the time whenever we 'put on our face' for a day at the office or transform ourselves in our 'glad rags' to let our hair down for a night out.

smack of smugness and complacency: the attitude that I am what I am and I don't need to bother about making any effort to be different' may actually be an expression of personal arrogant rather than, as we usually think, of humility.

Preoccupations with appearance and social behaviour may of course be viewed on a superficial level, but they are illustrative of deeper, less coherent striving. Before we can try to follow our destined way with confidence, we must know who we are and where we are going.

Appearance

Does the image that we present to the world matter? Are we the image others know or see or the image we think we know or see ourselves? To each their progress will be different, as new aspects become visible of the complete personality, the complete soul.

In my own early months of working with the spirits, I was given visions and pictures of what seemed to be a quite different 'me' during meditation sessions. I found myself going out of body in trance states, becoming increasingly aware of what I called my 'silver self' – probably my astral body - which had a different name to my earthly one. Journeying spontaneously into other realms, with no real knowledge at that time of any theories – shamanic or other – to explain what was going on, I simply placed my trust and faith in Mint and in the Source and allowed things to happen as they would.

I realised later that I was receiving constant instruction from Mist on the nature of self, particularly the difference between self-image and the reality of true self. In my own case I was being presented with working images that gave me awareness of an existence and a role — that reflected the description given in the opening quote to this chapter: apparently some kind of 'wise woman' with advanced insight and power. Not only that, but I was given the root sources from which this awareness sprang in a memory glimpse and vivid past life recall experienced round about the same time, which took me back to existence as a young woman of great spiritual awareness and authority – I thought at some time during the Roman occupation of Britain. I noted down immediately afterwards:

'It was a winter morning, the sky was blue and the sun was out and I was standing beside a lake wrapped in a long cloak. It was very wild and lonely, thick forest all around, everywhere covered in deep snow. There was somebody standing beside me, a man, but he was not important except as a familiar presence I felt comfortable with. I was contained within myself, exulting, laughing aloud with the joy of being there and of being aware with all my senses of my own being and the limitlessness of my links with the source of everything, filled with power. In that moment of awareness I saw a dark point move through the icy black water in front of me, spreading a clean arrow-like wake behind it. I knew it was an otter.'

Other information came from a source that was goddess-linked (in my case, I discovered afterwards, to a Romano-Celtic divinity called Sirona). I wrote later:

'When I first became aware of the Goddess and started getting channelled material from her, I experienced a kind of vision one day that was very clear, though completely unexpected. Alone in my flat, I 'saw' myself apparently out of my body and

with certainty (though I had no idea of what the ~~~~
was with myself), was some kind of goddess and the other was
some kind of priestess – though I could not be sure which was
which. I actually found it difficult to accept the vision at all,
even though a close friend to whom I described it later
assured me matter-of-factly that I was 'in the goddess role',
and added that of course, the High Priestess and the Goddess
were one and the same at certain times during ceremonies of
pagan worship.'

You cannot choose your destiny nor provide yourself with the
identity you would prefer, and your discovery of your true self
might not be what you expect, but you have to take what is
there, accept the 'who' that you are. In the city the scabs and
bones of life, the depths as well as the heights can be very
apparent, very in-your-face; urban life's habit of being
confrontationally shocking can help you make honest
assessments. Here, perhaps more than in the country, the
accelerated pace, the sharpness and focus of existence can
strip away pretence and pretension - and the acquiring of
wisdom and enlightenment is not a storing up of knowledge, it
is very much the opposite, a process of elimination, a
removing of veils and barriers to reveal the truth.

Though my own revelations were intensely meaningful to me,
the shamanic experience is universal, underlining the
interconnectedness of all living things. Individual vision may
seem essentially personal as we encounter it, but there is no
experience, no particular guide or tool the shaman can lay
claim to as 'his'. In order to fulfil his role he has let go the ego

and renounced all claim to 'mine' – so any other person, woman or man, may have exactly the same visions, experience exactly the same truths I did.

I felt very diffident about ever mentioning the experiences I have detailed above to anyone. I could not help feeling they might smack of an arrogant assumption that I was in some way superior to others who had never said anything about having visions of themselves wearing goddess cloaks. But recently I became unexpectedly enlightened when, while teaching a Psychic Development group, three of my students unconnectedly reported almost word for word the same experience. They too had 'seen' themselves as similar cloaked figures and come to awareness of their guides in just the same way it had happened to me.

I realised then that it was not arrogance, and I had not been suffering from delusions of grandeur. I had instead mistaken the significance of my visions, not realising they did not 'belong' to me and were not in some way marking me out. I saw they are the birthright of all: that all are equally parts of the divine, all equally favoured, equally honoured, of equal status.

Name

The novice, initiate, the aspirant on any spiritual path is likely to find himself the possessor of a new name bestowed in faith and intent as he sets out on his journey of discovery. Some religions, sects or cultures choose a name at random; in other cases, like the famous Apache warrior Geronimo, the name is bestowed because it is earned by personal achievement. Geronimo's name at birth was 'Goyahkla' (One Who Yawns), but he was given the name 'Geronimo' after he avenged the murder of his family so terribly in battle that his Mexican opponents prayed to St Geronimo to save them. The name, when it eventually arrives, might come from anywhere.

At some stage, I was not quite sure when or how, I was given a new name by Mist. It continued to be used over the years as my 'lessons' and dialogues proceeded, the inference being that this was the true name of my self, whether that self was the silver one which could fly into other worlds and dimensions, or the one that was holding conversations while sitting at the word processor. It was never spelled out, and so far as I could make it out phonetically, was written down when it occurred as AMAMOA.

Though I did not like it at first, finding it odd and unfamiliar to say, I spent a good deal of time trying to discover what it meant – or if it meant anything at all. Was it an endearment like the 'darling' that appeared often in the intimacy of our conversations? Was it some kind of title, symbolic of the work I was supposed to do? Was it a new word from some kind of higher dimension, or a word that actually existed, in some language I had never heard of?

The true, the final name which will eventually be the one by which we are known to the Source, is perhaps not one name but a series of them, a kind of identikit made up of bits and pieces from many different levels of existence, aspects of our personalities and our souls. Names can change, they need to change as circumstances and progress dictate, both in a physical and a spiritual connection. There can be hidden layers within a name, there can be ancestral, secret, power names which those who have the key can interpret and unravel. Our earthly names are of magical import, sacred and powerful, and yet in another way, they mean nothing. For they tell us only about other people – who our ancestors were, their physical colouring sometimes, their or our father's trade – or perhaps only the personal preference of our own parents. Who are we other all. We might well think, but the product of our surroundings, of those around us?

Years later, I chanced on several random discoveries that seemed to me of immense relevance regarding the new name I had been given and confirmed my initial impression that this, my 'true name', was simply an accurate description of the essence. I realised that 'my' name might be written down phonetically in other ways – for instance, as 'Amma-Mawu'. These two words are the names of primitive deities of African tribes: Amma a male creator god, Mawu a moon goddess (and also, in another connection, a sky god). Basically, the name might mean simply 'essential power of 'Man-Woman'.

I also discovered that the Chinese ideogram for 'I' might be described as 'a combination of the symbols for the Sun and Moon and their alternating and complementary qualities, a combination of the Yang and the Yin.' 'My' name reflects this, being simply another way of saying once again, 'essential quality and power of Sun-Moon', of the two polarities, Man-Woman.

When I had asked Mist for 'his' name, the answer that came was quite literal - simply a fact, 'I am mist'. And when I came to consider that 'my' name in spiritual work and in the great scheme of things might be a similar fact, one that in effect rubbed 'Me' out, reduced me to the basic elemental components of existence, took away the 'I' of self and left me apparently with no personality at all, reflecting simply a oneness, a participation in the whole, this seemed to me not only appropriate, but inevitable.

they used to perform their healing and rituals was much the same. In the tarot pack, the Wise Fool is generally pictured with a bundle slung over his shoulder – this too represents the medicine bundle, signifying empowerment through connection with outside forces.

Traditionally the shaman works with tools that intensify and underline his identification with the natural world. Rocks, pebbles, crystals are regarded as concentrations of power. Crystals, in some ancient tales, represent 'shattered truth', since the god Hercules dropped the crystal of truth while carrying it up Mount Olympus, and the fragments scattered in the form of smaller crystals through the world. Other shamanic traditions represent crystals as the tears or semen of sky spirits. Pebbles, leaves, plants or parts of animals all endowed the shaman with their particular properties, strengths and attributes.

Medicine and power objects are generally 'found' – 'given'. Country dwellers can discover the natural objects they need while walking the woods or the hills - feathers fallen from birds, weather-worn pieces of rock, tufts of sheep's wool caught on twigs or rough surfaces. Even perhaps, if you happened to be persistent enough, discarded snakeskin. But since the urban shaman – though very aware of the interconnectedness of all nature and in touch with the natural world – is not likely to need to intercede with the spirits for rain or follow the buffalo, his tools may be different, his needs dictating the sort of objects he will be able to use.

Walking the city streets, you can find your own personal and individual power objects in street markets, second-hand shops or auction sales. They will perhaps not come without some charge, but the charge is likely to be quite out of proportion to their inherent value. Among power objects I have collected over the years in this way are different replicas of gods, goddesses and divine beings known and unknown, in materials ranging from clay to wood to soapstone, in pictures of all kinds from water colours to oil paintings. Inspirational objects have included a circle of stained glass, painted stones, buckskin and beaded pouches and bags, carved candles, masks and woven cloths in beautiful Indian silk as well as natural cotton, glittering with tiny mirrors, a wooden carved platter.

Mysterious and powerful gem stones may also be found in broken and discarded bits of jewellry – I have rose quartz drops from a Victorian necklace, for instance, Edwardian onyx and agate eggs, even coloured glass charged with its own particular psychometric power.

The urban shaman need not go out and find crystals in their natural setting nor, unless he wants to, go to the trouble of making all his tools himself, though this is the traditional way. The city has its own gifts to offer, one of them being that the skills and loving handicrafts of others may add an extra blessing and intensified power to items that have been passed on over a period of time. In its way the city with its atmosphere of historical past can form as much of a communal unit as any nomadic tribe that rode together and carried its tents on the backs of its horses.

While the city is perhaps less obviously articulate in respect of natural beauty, the urban shaman will find his own special places where the voice of nature can be heard, and if he seeks humbly and in the right spirit, he will discover that the urban landscape abounds with gifts. In the rightful way, too, he can

Mindwork

Fat Girl (In the 'American')

- *through folds of virgin flesh*
⸻ ⸻, ⸻ ⸻ ⸻

- *lyric-fingered, touches a child,*
who laughs, seeing primroses
floating in her eyes;
- *nurse-laps dappled puppy*
in a podgy hand;

while through the petals,
reaches out to touch the greasy hair
of pony-tailed dream lover,

eying wispy Ophelia,
all legs in the corner,
drinking coffee,
red-smiling,
oozing
Tate and Lyle.

PG

At some time or another, most seekers along the spiritual path will face the problems of trying to clarify both their identity and their role. Who and what am I, actually? What part do I have to play in the greater scheme of things? In just this way I too wondered how to describe myself when I had to (as it were) present my credentials, particularly in regard to the new work I was beginning to do: I was a writer and novelist, yes, but this did not seem to be particularly relevant to the fact that I now gave psychic counsel. So what was I, in fact? A clairvoyant – a tarot reader – a healer - ? All the lot – or something else?

asking questions, I was eventually able to appreciate the secret of shamanic living – that you do not need to understand yourself or what you are. 'Self', the ego, is abandoned in order to proceed to awareness of that 'true self' of which all are a part.

I have learned to be chary of claims made, statements asserted when they involve cosmic missions or assumptions of divine identity/destiny. During one of my spells in a psychiatric hospital – long before I had any real idea of psychic awareness - I had a salutary experience. One of the patients prosaically helping me to wash my hair in a washbasin revealed in confidence that she was actually 'a Bride of Christ'. She was guided by heavenly voices, this sweet, faded little lady said, which had revealed to her that she had a mission to kill to rid the world of ungodly people.

Now more familiar with clinical illnesses like paranoid schizophrenia and 'religious mania', as well as various types of mediumship, I have had to learn – sometimes very frighteningly and unexpectedly - to recognise the difference between dangerous delusional states and genuine cases of psychic or supernatural enlightenment/possession/power. In genuine cases of divine destiny, the person concerned will suffer great doubt and find it difficult to accept whatever high status he seems to have been appointed, continually seeking to re-evaluate, question and clarify, fearing all the time he is 'going mad'. It is the truly deluded who never queries his own sanity.

tests of faith, nothing but an inflexible statement, then it is likely to be something that does need to be questioned.

If some kind of apparently destined role is involved, it is especially difficult to view the situation objectively. The following dialogues will I hope illustrate my own bewilderment in this respect – and though the images I was given were personal and comforted me, they might well have been universally given, equally applicable to anyone else in need of such reassurance.

Reading and meditation

The reality – in conversation with mist

1

I do not feel I should listen to the others, but am I being arrogant?
- *Confusion is always dark.*
- *You walk a different way.*
- *(More emphatically) Know your worth and act upon it. From this moment revive the stars about your neck – they will cure the aching (smiles) - and the jewel between your breasts. Also the star sign within the Third Eye. Your weapons lie rusting in the cases. Would you go forth from a king's court or the forest telling those who met you to ignore you and your words? (Angry, exasperated) Even so in a city or a room. You take your forest your court, your cave with you. Your cloak is known and will protect you.*

Thank you.

- Unworthiness when assumed in one so great is a double arrogance. Lesser than yourself cannot lift you nor encourage you. They do not understand the burdens. You must lift yourself by your own needs. If it was not one person it would be another, these are foolish matters and must be left alone or you will tangle yourself in petty bitternesses like barbed wire. Free yourself and walk the forest, the mountain. Shine. Be. Your shining depends on no-one. Their shining is irrelevant to you. You are of the mist, of us, remember and recognise your calling.

Thank you. I will.

2

Mist my dear one, I need your advice, I do not know what to do.

- If in doubt, do nothing.

But is it possible without continuing to feel as low as I do?

- That is up to you.

It seems that I have been trying to get things right for a long time and I cannot feel in control or as though I have the right to decide for myself, you know how I have tried.

- My dear one I know. But there is no need. You have learned for yourself that it is enough to Shine and Be.

It's all very well when one is just thinking on high planes, it doesn't seem to work with ordinary things.

- The choice is yours, my dear one. You may if you wish remain like the rest.

But I don't feel as though I have got dignity, self-respect, let alone a high spirit.

- Your feelings are not fact.

How will this work out? I want to free myself from all my difficult circumstances, and even feelings.

- Transfer the focus, fill your life with other things.

You are right, as you always are.

Will I ever get myself together in this life, or will it be a struggle all the time?

- Let go of the struggle. Shine. Be. There is a place for you and you are in it. Do not thresh around and try to find another. Take the blessing, my darling child, walk simply and tall.
I understand, darling Mist. The rest does not matter, does it?
- Only if you let it. You are named, you have been given your place and called.
What about my problems, will they go away?
(silence)
Should I try to get rid of them?
- Shift the focus, the energy.
I over-react, I know.
- Why not? You have your rights as a living creature to live.
I understand dear Mist, thank you.

3

Mist my darling I seem to have gone a long way from you, are you with me? I know you are, but I must have been closer to the Earth than you. What shall I do about the book?
   - You are the Wise Woman.
I can't keep up with your thoughts. Will my book be okay? Is it what was intended?
   - Speak your truth and that is enough.
Yes, I feel that. If I start gathering material together, will that do?
- Too positive a query my darling, you deal with mist.
Can you give me a message now, as a sign?
(Pause)
- The mountains of the moon are desolate and empty, but there are holes in time, where the past was and is no longer. Those who were shining shine no more in your eyes and their

147

shadows exist only, but no substance to cast those shadows.
- And yet they speak through you. The truth stands, it is
enough, there is no need of more. Listen well, child.

Thank you darling Mist.
Come closer, I miss you.
- And I you.
But you seem - .
- Seem?
You ARE, but am I? Am I enough, myself?
- I am.
You are greater than me.
- If you say so.
I'm sorry, I have lost the touch. (There had been no
communication for some time.)
- No way.
Be powerful, be strong (for me).
- Those are your qualities now.
I can't believe it. I would rather you were the great shining
one. I am not half so glamourous.
- It's a tough rough business my darling, no glamour. JC had
dirty feet.
I have wounds, marks (operation scars), the debris of a life so
far.
- Let them go.
I will.
- Fly my darling, believe in your wings.
Glorious, and I can sense you with me.
- I am always with you.
Let me never forget that.
- Forget or not, it does not make any difference. I do not
change.
What about the fading and dying, if I do? (referring to
previous communications)
- I die but I do not change. I am if you believe in me.
Are you god?
   (Mist laughs)

148

(I sensed great tolerance)
- *Do not ask questions. I cannot answer. Do not ask questions.*
 (I was referring to a book called *Talking With Angels* in the next speech)
The angels say there is to be no asking 'why'. Must I not ask 'why'?
- *Ask, if you wish.*
(After some thought) I have nothing to ask. I am content.
- *You have your answer, my darling.*
'Darling' seems wrong here, this conversation is business. Shall I use another name? Amamoa? (This had been mentioned before)
- *Amamoa of the starry hair.*
- *child of dark and light,*
- *spring of my delight,*
- *tree of my strength,*
- *pathway for my feet,*
- *red sun of my dawn,*
- *light of my dying eyes,*
- *water of my thirst,*
- *dream of winter,*
- *vision of spring.*
Those are very beautiful.
- *That is Amamoa.*
Then business is the same as pleasure?
- *If you make it so.*
I understand. Thank you my darling Mist, that is wonderful. Is it the same for all?
- *If they dare, if they aspire.*
They will be glad. Thank you.
- *Enough.*

helped me to learn to search ~~deeply~~ delusion. There are many different types of delusion and often these too are deeply hidden.

Many 'wannabe shamans' can see no connection between scientific or clinical theory and natural inspiration. But all learning is valuable, whatever the source and whether between the covers of textbooks or 'written in the wind and water'. Read a few basic books on self-help, even psychology, to discover how the mind works in this respect, or attend a crash course or evening classes.

2 Give yourself and your life a 'make-over', whether mental, physical or both. Treat yourself to 'make-overs' from different experts and enjoy them as you let the 'true you' emerge in all its different facets.

3 Start collecting objects that reflect your feelings about yourself and your work and use them in your every day living.

4 Are you still keeping your written record of progress?

Chapter 8

The Wounded Healer

May it be beautiful before me
May it be beautiful behind me
May it be beautiful all around me
In beauty may I walk
In beauty it is finished.
> Navajo healing chant, the '*Blessed Way*', concluding lines

Humour has been described as potentially one of the finest forms of thought and perception. It is a human necessity.
> John Southworth
> *Fools and Jesters at the English Court*

When you recognise your pain is unimportant in the greater scheme of things, you are able to let it go
> Yvaine Huath

A writer knows there are certain rules in fiction. Heroes and heroines are allowed to suffer from illness but it has to be of an acceptable type: they would cease being heroic the minute they succumbed to nosebleeds/adenoids or admitted having in-growing toenails, for instance, and the experienced novelist makes certain that they are never laid low by anything other than perhaps a faint or fever, or possibly (in order to further the plot) a ricked ankle.

refuse to take them into account;
image you feel happy to show the world if conscious of falling
short of the heroic ideal.

As a healer it is especially difficult to explain to others, or
even justify to yourself, why you may not be a perfect
specimen, why you cannot heal your own problems and pain,
and during the years when I worked as a psychic and healer
in London this was something of which I was very conscious.
Through no fault, I reminded myself repeatedly, of my own I
was overweight for my height, shapeless and bloated because
of the medication I had to take, unable to move easily because
of my back pain - and then there were those other, more
embarrassing physical problems I tried hard to laugh off. Let's
face it, they hampered my confidence to a crippling degree.

I wanted to look appropriate to work which was very much in
the public domain. People who consulted me needed to be able
to feel they could have confidence in my authority, trust my
judgement. But it was difficult (dare I say, impossible even?)
to look remotely glamorous in shapeless kaftans, hard to feel I
could maintain any kind of mystique as a representative of
higher aspiring or spiritual enlightenment; on-going gynaecol-
ogical difficulties rubbed out all sense of being attractively
feminine, and no woman feels she can transcend menopausal
embarrassments while actually experiencing those crippling
'sweats', 'flushes' and the emotional vulnerability that accom-
panies this 'rite of passage'. None of this seemed to bother the
people who consulted me. But it did bother me. How was I to
rationalise my sense of shameful adequacy that, while
counselling and healing others, I was falling apart myself?
One very hot week in summer I was attending a Fair at a

holistic centre in Southern England, manning a bookstall in a marquee which, beneath the baking sun and with no cooling breezes able to penetrate, was daily transformed into what might well have passed for some kind of sweat lodge. Sitting on the campstool we had brought, I suffered agonies of discomfort and embarrassment, stifled, uncomfortable and hating myself. What a contrast to the woman at the next stall, who though actually slightly older than me, looked years younger. Appearing each day in shorts and a brief top, slim, blonde and cool, she would stretch herself on her yoga mat out of sight of her customers and go through her meditation rituals, breathing easily and moving her body supply. She told me reassuringly: 'I was like you once. But don't worry. One day, you will be like me.'

I did not believe her. My seemingly everlasting 'mid-life' symptoms had been going on for years; in addition, several doctors (one a Harley Street consultant) had said that the damage to my spine was irreversible, short of surgical intervention with no guarantee of success. So, no chance of a miracle 'back replacement'. I knew – and told my friend – that I would never be even remotely slender again, never supple or free from disabling health problems. I would probably be on pain-killers for the rest of my life.

She just smiled.

This story is an allegory. It is not concerned with how – or even whether - my own health improved, but with the nature of shamans. I had always assumed they had to be extremely fit physically: they undertook strenuous feats of endurance, after all, were powerfully built, imposing in their strength and presence, their bodies extensions of their minds, disciplined and controlled, not burdens that dragged them down.

especially when getting on in ~~~~~~~~~~~~~~~~~~~~~~~~~~~~~~~~~
myself. A shaman, as inspired visionary and spiritual leader
of his people, is also physically inspirational. Glowing with
health, tramping the trails, untiring, in harmony with
everything in nature, never a problem or a care. Or at least,
that was what I thought.

I was to learn, some years later, that I had got it all wrong.

Teaching of Red Elk and Grey Elk

Enlightenment came after I paid a visit to a friend, a fellow-
psychic I had worked with and trusted, who generously put
me up in her very busy household on a mattress on her living-
room floor for the night. As I lay there half-asleep, I became
aware of a presence in the room with me. It was the very
definite and physically impressive figure of a Native
American Indian who, having made sure I knew he was there,
proceeded to squat down cross-legged beside me as though he
intended to keep watch through the night. I was surprised
even though I knew Rosemarie had long-standing connections
with Native American guides – even more so when he still
seemed to be present in the morning. He did not appear to
want to speak, so I asked Rosemarie if she could give me any
explanation. She said simply: 'He's come to take care of you.'

She also revealed, while doing a reflexology session on my
feet, that she was being told 'the elders' were with me. I had
had no overtly shamanic guidance or connection before, and
was inclined to treat the sudden appearance of 'my' Indian
brave with some suspicion, but he remained – and has
remained – more or less present ever since, often assisting me

silently during sessions of healing. I have many times been aware of seeing him working on the patients on my therapy couch while I am working on them myself, performing healing rituals that involve leaves, plants, even painted face and body markings and symbols, that I know nothing of but which are fascinating to witness. Most healers work with healing guides of some kind and I had brief experience in the early days of working with someone I called 'the Eskimo doctor', but I never imagined my principal partner would turn out to be an Indian brave. A case of poetic justice, perhaps, in view of my previous attitude towards shamans.

In my book *Come Shining Through,* written soon after 'my' Indian had appeared to me, I noted:

'He is around if I need him but mainly he appears when I am working with Reiki (the healing discipline I use). He works with me, sometimes taking over my hands as the 'Eskimo doctor' used to do. On other occasions I am aware of him carrying out his own healing rituals alongside me, in the process of which I am given vivid images of the way he viewed his country, the landscape and the animals of North America. I also receive insights into the methods used by his tribe for healing.

'I have not yet managed to discover the tribe to which he belonged but his name is Red Elk. There is a kind of shamanic link with another, much older member of his tribe too, but this man does not reveal himself fully. I am aware of the still figure sitting quietly cross-legged in the shadows, too frail to walk but radiating spiritual power. Because the name I get for him is Grey Elk, I assume these two were probably related – perhaps Grey Elk was a shaman, a medicine man who passed on his teachings to his son or grandson.

'Though I would love to know more about them I am content to wait until they decide to let me discover further details in part of each other.'

I still do not know the tribe to which they belong, but during the intervening years I have begun to appreciate some of the lessons they wanted to teach me. Red Elk, young and fit, with the litheness and strength one might expect in a shaman, appears in sharp contrast to the physical frailness, the bodily weakness of the 'elder' Grey Elk. Which is the shaman? And why are they both present?

I can see now that they are both equal in stature, parts of the same whole. That youthful strength is necessary in order to undertake and endure the difficult lessons and trials that will result in the old man's wisdom and knowledge, housed in a feebler – even a damaged or wounded - frame. It is this concept that makes for the traditional training of a novice by the adept, why the shaman's knowledge has to be passed on to the young pupil by the master.

There must be challenge or there can be no growth. But growth is painful, sometimes seemingly unbearably painful. In the tarot pack the cards which deal with such aspects of living all reveal its pain. The Moon card in particular, which signifies spiritual growth, usually depicts a narrow path passing between two towers, guarded by fearsome-looking beasts. While dragging itself from the primal waters of its earthly awareness, the soul must dare to tread that path and suffer the terrors of a strange dark country roamed by huge beasts beneath the shadow of the moon.

The shaman learns not to fear failure, suffering and death but to accept the shadows, the dark side of existence, to balance each against the other. Personal pain has to be acknowledged and accepted before it can be let go, in recognition that the journey is greater than the individual undertaking it. Acceptance is a vital part of the healing process, willingness to submit to the spiritual lessons involved, to relinquish the over-riding assumptions and fears of the ego and allow individual pain to be sacrificed as part of a much deeper and greater anguish. By being willing to face it if we have to, in spite of the fear, we invalidate the original pain so that it ceases to be an enemy and works instead as an ally, a teacher.

It is when the individual obsessively dwells in his fear, holding on to his pain or using it negatively, inflicting it on both himself and others for the wrong reasons – as a weapon of punishment or revenge, of self loathing or even of sheer despair and a need for help – that the balance is tipped the wrong way. The Native American Indians, as a part of their heritage, not only accepted failure and death, they celebrated it as something positive rather than negative - perhaps it would make for better health and living if we could all do this. For again we see the empowering strength of acceptance and surrender.

At the massacre of Sand Creek, near Denver, on 29th November 1864, when Black Kettle led the Cheyenne and Arapaho against the army and the death count was 28 men and 105 women and children, it was reported that another Chief, White Antelope, 'refused to fight or flee. He stood in front of his tipi and sang his death song

'Nothing lives long
Except the earth and the mountains'

until he was killed.'

Another example of this was in 1871, when the Kiowa Chief Datan? was being taken to Texas to be tried for murder. During the journey he too, while manacled hand and foot, began singing his death song

*'O sun you remain for ever, but we Ko-eet-senko must die
O earth you remain for ever, but we Ko-eet-senko must die'.*

Shadow of the Moon

The aspiring shaman – or anyone who is growing and progressing - actually needs such roundness of experience and may well feel frustrated without knowing the reason if never allowed to try or test his growing strengths, mental and physical, in the kind of celebrations and challenges that make up 'rites of passage' towards an increasing maturity. Primitive peoples intuitively understood this, though accounts of warrior initiations and so on in native societies can often seem barbarous to over-civilised western eyes: they helped prepare the novice for the dark side of living, equipping him to deal with seemingly negative aspects of existence like pain and death.

There is an unspoken conspiracy of wishful thinking in our age of scientific wonders, based on the assumption that ideally, there ought to be no suffering, pain or indeed anything remotely unpleasant in the world. These, it is felt, are 'the enemy' which must be challenged and overcome. In the Utopia we aspire to there will be no illness, no ageing, no dying: everyone will live for ever with absolutely nothing to worry about, on one long stress-free holiday.

'Illness' is generally visualised as a bad thing, the opposite of 'wellness', which is the only good. And many aspirants to spiritual or even shamanic living, with no awareness of the significance of the dark depths that exist alongside the heights, have no real desire – at least, not yet - to explore concepts like the Jungian 'Shadow' or turn up crawlies under the stones within their own personalities. This is understand-able, but a willingness to try to know and embrace one's own pain, one's own sullen and cowering 'Shadow', is just as necessary for the novice as aspiring towards the light of one's Higher Self or selves.

As in the natural world, the shaman lives only in the moment of awareness, trusting in the power of the universal Source to sustain him. Animal nature exists largely day by day - and in spite of all the effort and energy that might be expended, does worry really help? Will all the worry in the world stop the dawn from coming or the sun from rising? Troops in battle learn it makes life easier and more bearable if you believe the bullet with your name on it will get you, and there is not a great deal you can do beyond take sensible precautions. Only a certain amount can be achieved by 'free will', the rest is predestined, out of our control, and there can be no cast-iron 'security' or guarantees of anything in this life.

The shamanic nature is fluid, flexible as the elements. When dealing with trauma, it is often the refusal to expand, to metamorphose, to change and develop and grow, that is the cause of illness and trouble. Individuals may have become 'stuck' at some stage in their development, made an unconscious decision as a result of pressures of the past, (nearly always in childhood), which holds them back. For instance, never to succeed in a material sense, however much they think they want to, simply because their mother/father so desperately wanted this outcome. Many of the situations the healer/shaman encounters are familiar to psychologists and can be found in textbooks. The problems are the same, the shaman may simply 'see' another way of addressing them.

Our problems and pain are often created by the ego's frantic efforts to take control, its refusal to listen to what the universe is trying to tell us. Even when dealing with the spirits of the dead, the medium/shaman often finds that the living - the mourners - will not let the departed spirit go, their violent grief and refusal to accept that death has occurred preventing it from being able to move forward.

The mirror-image of the shaman's vision sees beyond self, beyond personal feeling and emotion. It sees what is there, accepts things as they are – that weakness and frailty is not an acknowledgement of failure, that loss and pain are not the greatest threats nor death the terrifying end it may appear, some extreme manifestation of all the perceived 'enemy' can inflict.

Places where the dead lie can be the most peaceful on earth, and not necessarily just consecrated ground, the hallowed atmosphere of a graveyard. While researching a novel about the First World War, I visited Ypres and the surrounding countryside – having also written about more ancient battles and explored their sites at various times in my career – and though not then aware of psychic ability, was moved to uncontrollable tears. I believe now that it was my personal assumption of pity and sorrow for what might have occurred in these places, rather than any genuine psychometric or atmospheric 'message', that prompted my outpouring of grief: when I learned later to simply connect with what I was given rather than try to 'imagine' scenarios myself, I found I received unexpectedly different information.

I have consciously connected with the departed dead during the moments of silence on Armistice Day over the last few years, and to my surprise the messages that came through were overwhelmingly of upliftment, of joy and empowerment, not of sorrow or grief. 'There was no loss, no defeat, none of it was wasted,' is the reassurance overwhelmingly, strongly given. I found this difficult to take – did it mean that war was justified, I wondered? But it was not the wars as such that were being referred to, it was the striving, the transcendental endeavour of all the human spirits who fought on whatever side, the overwhelming efforts to try and uphold ideals, however misguided, of loyalty, trust, duty, faithfulness and an honest sense of 'right'.

I have never visited the sites of former concentration camps but it would not be surprising if the suffering and pain endured there had in some way clouded the atmosphere – not necessarily the suffering and pain itself, but the dark of beings who, for whatever reason, allowed such atrocities to happen and carried them out. Yet the torment can sometimes be more that of the torturer than of his victim, and the shaman recognises this, for it is only by accepting the completeness of the unity of dark/light, suffering/lack of suffering that he is able to achieve – albeit in rare glimpses – that sense of utter identification with, and absorbing into the perfect cosmic soul: the soul that perceives it is in the end the choice made to embrace the dark, the choice made to accept the inflicting of suffering on even the smallest creature, that is the ultimate evil.

This is not some undefined emotional concept, it is the fact of his own suffering that gives the shaman, beyond all else, his authority and power to confront suffering in others. We are what we choose to embody within ourselves, and if we accept the whole spectrum of our existence without becoming polarised, we are balanced and complete, unified and at peace within. In accepting suffering, accepting whatever cruelty and pain may be inflicted without becoming obsessed by whatever has caused it, or by human desires for revenge, the spirit will soar and rise to unbelievable heights, transcending all else. This is the lesson we are perhaps to learn from a consideration of suffering and pain – that it teaches us, if we will be taught, how to rid ourselves not of pain but of an awareness of pain; that only by accepting it can we invalidate it and cause it to cease to exist.

The shaman, as a healer, a medicine man, oversaw and expedited all aspects of living, dying and rites of passage in this world and in Otherworlds, the physical and the spiritual well being of his people. His working knowledge had to encompass something of natural medicine, herbalism, counselling, practicalities of dealing with all types of illness, as well as the secrets of magic, divination, mediumship and seership. He could and did perform 'cures' that were often seemingly miraculous. Yet his first duty, as a healer, was to himself and his own wholeness. Though the shaman's life may be a series of journeys that take him into other worlds besides this one - to make requests on behalf of others, to assist others to be healed, to retrieve lost and trapped souls in his role as a 'psychopomp', a guide and conductor of the souls of the dead to their rightful place - essentially and most important of all, he seeks wisdom, enlightenment and healing on his own behalf, his spiritual journey continually ongoing.

I discovered that my search for identity was not so that I could reveal the answer, when I found it, to an interested public but so that I could, by attempting to know myself more truly and fully, discover the potential that lay within my own being and live more truthfully and fully myself.

To all who tread the shaman's or the healer's path, trials and lessons come in different ways. I tried to come to terms with what I felt were my personal physical limitations in the meditations, life path workings and writing I did during those London years. Though I knew many healers and was having various treatments at different clinics and hospitals, nothing seemed to actually change the physical being I now was, and I told myself I had been given my various illnesses for a reason. I even thought I knew what it was.

People would say: 'If Dawn can do it, in her state, then I can.' So I made jokes myself to encourage sitters to go forward. 'Look at me,' I'd say to gorgeous women who had no confidence. 'If you think I manage to look good, what about you? What have you got to worry about?'

So was that it? Had I been given my health problems so that I could use them constructively, be a kind of example and yardstick, act as an inspiration? I wrote the following notes at one stage, trying to find a pattern, make sense of the lessons I was being taught, discover confidence in myself. They did comfort me very much at the time.

All those years ago, seeming gone in the blink of an eye, a small Welsh girl with hills and sky and grass and water flowing in her hair and the vision in her eyes, saw and recognised the call. She set out to find it, the vision and the dream.

Today I see the light clearer on the water, the sky higher, the grass more real, and the whole encased within a glass bubble that, if shaken, produces snowflakes to drift out of an afternoon sky onto a deserted bridge, a man watching. (This was a clear memory of one intense, ecstatic moment of transcendent experience in my twenties with DHS, a man I was intimately close to for ten years. We had driven to Llangollen in North Wales one Christmas Eve and I stood on the bridge there with snow starting to fall, in a instant of awareness that crystallised into something magical I never afterwards forgot. I did not know then – and would never have believed – that DHS was going to emerge years later as one of my spirit guides. I doubt very much whether he had any inkling of such a possibility either.)

I must keep the glass and turn it occasionally but remember that lost loves, lost youth, lost fevers and friends, are past and cannot go forward into old age. No use talking about Time. Youth is a different country as well as the past. (A reference to L P Hartley's opening sentence of *The Go-Between* – 'The past

is a different country, they do things differently there'.)
The present is only hindered by constant referral to the past. Let each moment possess its own excitement, its own freshness and promise. It has never happened before and will never come again. One day I will look back on this morning and see myself as - .

A red-haired virago who passes, unknowingly famous among the crowds with great achievements behind me, someone who loves me though in his way which is difficult, tremblingly holding to my spirit in the face of the body's abysses, still going forward. Someone who, if that small girl had met her, might have been her heroine, to protect and defend.

How strange, the child defending the woman, that little person who never knew how to live. Notta.

The shamanic vision is intensely practical and too honest to suffer fools gladly. As well as our destined trials, we have been given reasoning power and plain common sense. There is nothing particularly praiseworthy about putting up with any pain or suffering if it can be avoided: if there are means at our disposal to cure ills or avoid them, we would be foolish not to make use of them, whatever they are.

An appreciation of our intrinsic individual worth will enable us to stand our ground, recognise our right to existence. With effort we assert our will to control our fate, our willingness to try and make progress. Without it we would stagnate or even go backwards. And even so far as attempting to heal the problems and ills of others, encouraging them with truths they will – for the moment, for whatever reason – perhaps be unable to accept, that too needs to be done, however futile it appears. We are only human, we will never know when the moment will come that the truth suddenly becomes blazingly apparent and the individual concerned will burst free and find himself on the path, his way clear ahead.

There are different kinds of 'illness' that the healer will encounter and some can only be cured by the natural world itself, if at all. If you should be crushed beneath the force of a falling tree or trapped by lava from an erupting volcano, these are natural disasters that are purely physical and cannot be anticipated by any kind of preventative medicine – though you might perhaps have been advised to keep out of the danger area. Broken bones cannot be made whole again, but can only be encouraged to mend: other problems are caused by imbalance and strain, when muscles, for example try to compensate for injury and in doing so create further problems that put the whole body out of balance, under such stress it cannot function effectively.

Inevitably, in spite of all our efforts, some pain will remain, and in many cases, seemingly unfair, unbearable agonising pain. It is only with an over-view that the patterns of meaning can be perceived, that what comes into being as a result of suffering and pain can be appreciated. We cannot

know in the midst of our suffering what the end result will prove to be, what is actually being born, what new self will emerge created by our willingness to endure and be strong. We are unable in our pain to appreciate that any answer exists to the question of why it is there, far less one that will satisfy us or make any sense we can understand.

Love

put out both my eyes
blind
I feel my way

Yet onward creep
And do not look behind
Though dark my fiercest day

All lost, no rest but in my grave,
All gone, hope spent, breath taken,
Worms' food, fear's fool, by life itself forsaken
I die and wake to

Love

DG

Mindwork

I come to speak to you
I am tying you to the wind
Let the passing spirits come here
to help us
to relieve the illness
of your servant

Part of the healing oration of a
contemporary Mayan curandero

The breath we breathe is the most basic necessity of life and
the sounds we can make with our breath are magical. Ancient
Egyptians believed that the gods Thoth and Ptah carried out
creation solely by the sound of their voices; the Indian Shiva
did the same thing to the sound of a rattle held in one hand.
Sacred chant reflects this vital and magical property of air
and breath.

The word inspiration means both drawing breath in, and
receiving divine influence. The Roman writer Cornelius
Agrippa commented on how the shaman would chant over a
sick person in such a way that his breath would flow over the
patient – in a similar way perhaps, gamblers blow on the dice
for luck. When we hear that the healers of Epidaurus placed
their patients in the middle of the amphitheatre and set up a
rolling vibration around them, we are reminded again of the
shaman's traditional connections with theatre, his role as
Entertainer – the actor, acting out new scenarios, creating
new worlds in the consciousness of his audience. Other
traditional ancient healing practices like those of the Chinese
and the Maya, lay great emphasis on temperature, air and
wind.

The shaman heals by keeping our breath flowing in tune with
the vibrations and sounds of the natural world, by restoring
the sick person to a harmonious state within the whole of

existence. All shamanic healing works on the principles of wholeness, but not just the wholeness of one individual, the corporate wholeness of all.

The Native Indian concept of the Medicine Wheel forms a cross within a circle. It signifies that we begin our life's journey at birth in the east at dawn ' a place of light and new beginnings'; the south is consolidation, innocent self-expression and joy, the place of the child; in the west lies fruition, the place of the adult, where we develop intuition and imagination and suffer the pain of growth. The north is wisdom, the place of calm reflection, the place of the elder. We have a purpose, moving constantly, traversing the wheel until we are able to leave off journeying and achieve what we have been seeking all along – the still centre, the point of unity and calm.

'Wellness' or 'illness' are not polarised, fixed points. You cannot stop or reach any end while your life is in progress. Neither can you choose where to begin, you must begin within the here and now, with what you have and what you are. 'I am looking for peace,' people often tell me. Or happiness. Or even, often, security. Their misconception is that these are states to be arrived at, that once they manage to get there, their lives will never again contain anything bad, there will be no disasters or unexpected problems and nothing will be able to touch them. In fact they are negating the whole idea and purpose of existence. All living things are in constant state of movement, whether the particles in a sub-atomic dance or the soul feeling its way in fear and trembling along a dark path.

'I just want to be free,' people say to me often, yet while honestly believing they want nothing more than 'to be free', fighting every inch of the way against anyone and anything they see as restraining or confining them, most individuals nevertheless fear complete freedom and the personal responsibilities it carries with it. Like peace, like security, freedom – or even happiness or content - is not what we commonly imagine it to be.

The shaman's vision of wholeness is of harmony and balance, no beginning and no end to the journey. It sees the beauty in all things, recognises that all things are equal.

Reading and meditation
The breath of life; Words of Brother Gregory

1

Can we compare in beauty with the singing stars in the sky of midnight? No, for our path is low and cruel and the songs of the stars are not for us. But can the stars in their pristine purity sing of the joy of lifting another from the mire, whether he be a crying child, or a man with sores and the red eyes of weariness and lack of hope, or a woman clumsy and extended with a child she is too weak to bear?

Oh my children, even as you forget to be good and extend your hands to another in compassion and love, and share what you have because you cannot enjoy your fortune peacefully while others have nothing, they will value your crumbs as the glorious gift of meat with pastry and roasting pheasant and sucking pig. So your song will rise through the layers of the cosmos and be heard by God, though you know nothing of it. For the good life is not lived consciously. If you are aware of your own goodness, you have become entombed within it as though it was a grave.

Live your life to the full as the butterfly lives its bright day, and the gnat lives its evening of rich light, and the glow-worm lives its moment of glory. That is all the goodness that is required of you.

2

You speak of happiness, child. But to each, his happiness must be his own creation. For we build our happiness as a master built this abbey, stone by stone; and not the stones of the earth only but the stones of the mind and the stones of intent and generosity and self-sacrifice.

See the abbey walls, how they soar, the buttresses and the towers. But where have they come from, my child? From the mind of the architect who saw them before they existed or from the hands of the workmen who carefully placed the stones, or from the vision complete which we see with our eyes and which lifts us to God?

A smile is happiness, child, one stone of the abbey that is for you to build, and a word of kindness is another, and the sense of joy in the simplicity of your daily round will build the staircase to the belfry.

What are the bells to sing out and proclaim your happiness? My voice, you tell me, but it is not so, your voice cannot speak true only your heart, and your heart will sing out the call to matins and vespers so that the country people who hear will come to the place where your heart sings in accompaniment to their own.

But child, these are small matters, happiness and joy, what are they all but crumbs from God's table, and all the while His feast is spread and you may enter in as an honoured guest. But there, you learn with every day that passes, and in your very self you carry happiness in the fleet grace and bright air of your youth. I am old in spite of my wisdom and your sunlight is happiness to me child, and welcome to my old bones. You do not know how you give joy to others even in the fact of your own existence.

In conversation with Mist

Mist my darling, one of my greatest problems is fear. Can you help me with this? I am always afraid, more especially now, of illness and pain.

- Are you sure?

Well, I think so. I do get panic attacks, heart palpitations, all the physical symptoms of stress - . But I can see even as I am telling you this, my higher self knows I am not talking about fear but awareness of my human condition.

- You are meant to be whole. When a part is unbalanced comes the pain.

That's all very well, but it hurts.

- I am amazed. (Gentle sarcasm)

I am a child again, trying to tell you what you already know. And I am losing the fear now.

- Is that not what you wanted?

Yes, but how can I feel like this what I get the panic and attacks?

- Become aware.

Of you?

- Of everything. Fear confines.

You are right, it is true.

- Expand.

Mentally or physically?

- Breathe, expand the lungs, enlarge the moment of sensation. Allow all to

penetrate not just a little.

Mist, you are so wise. Should I not fear pain and illness, then?

- Fear has its part to play, otherwise there would be no fear.

What about pain and illness?

- Do you experience them now?

No. Not at this moment, not unless I look for them.

- There is your answer, my darling.

But when I do experience them, when I had surgery and that terrible toothache - . It is unbearable.

- You bore it and survived.

I can remember it, though. It existed.

- *So did birth.*
That is a strange thing to say.
- *Why so? Birth is your greatest suffering.*
You mean if I had not been born, I would not suffer at all?
- *Even so.*
Well, I suppose that's true, I would not be human, I would be – like you? But was I sent here only to suffer?
- *To survive it and so overcome it.*
Death will be a release, then?
- *An unlocking of the prison door.*
But why, Mist? What is my life for? What is human existence all about?
- *You will question.*
Is that necessary?
- *Nothing is stationary, all progresses.*
From where, to where? (Silence) I suppose you won't tell me.
- *If I told you, would you be any better off? (Smiling)*
No, I suppose not, but I'd know, at least.
- *Knowledge is not an end in itself.*
What about truth?
- *Truth is. Knowledge assists.*
You're right. I am too clever by half.
- *You shine. That is good.*
It's wonderful to be back 'at school', learning. When you have become educated here, you think that is it. No further to go, only explorations in different directions. Instead, the whole process happens again, doesn't it, like a child starting over from the beginning.
- *Nature renews itself. So do you.*
That's wonderful.
- *Enough, my little scholar. Rest now. You are tired. Too fast is as bad as too slow.*
Thank you, my darling teacher. I will.

Practical

The urban shaman is fortunate because he is more likely to have access to a wide range of educative tools than the country dweller. Make use of facilities offered – from the libraries and museums already mentioned to courses and classes where you may be able to explore different healing disciplines. Examine them all, from crystals to 'hands on' and faith healing, homeopathy to conventional medicine. Particularly try to become familiar with healing methods that may be completely alien to your own experience - in some countries even today, people can become ill, or even die, as a result of what they perceive as 'the evil eye' or 'bad spirits'. The modern day shaman, offered such richness of information, recognises the usefulness of every cultural system and from his questioning and learning will evolve his own particular style and truth. You may find it helpful to build up a reference library, and always keep notes.

Chapter 9

Travelling Vertically: Into Other Worlds

We Ride on Ahead

absent body thoughts
riding horses
transpire a nimbus kingdom,
wafted by the smile of Azrael,
death's black angel,
seated on high mounds,

as word tones smash
towards the sensual glimpse
of golden domes and mists
of moonlit city,
where time-drops surge
like horses' hooves.

disorientated...
via ether voices,
we squeeze a gelding dawn.

PG

The shamans travelled vertically

Tom Chetwynd
Dictionary of Sacred Myth

The otherworlds that shamans journey to are many and varied and can encompass any number of features, because each is a construct of the shaman that enters it.

William Adcock
Shamanism

Enjoy the journey – there may not be an end to reach
Yvaine Huath

Shamans work in different worlds and on different levels. The shamanic view of existence brings us back to the concepts of nature, the cosmos often being represented as a great tree, mythologically called the World Tree, that encompasses Upper World, Middle World and Lower or Underworld. A tree with its roots in the earth, its growth through atmosphere and its branches in the air, the cloud, represents different states of mind, different perceptions of living. It is symbolic of an existence that is multi-dimensional, aspirational yet firmly rooted, psychologically representing conscious, subconscious and unconscious activity.

By whatever means, the empowered person is able to visit these Otherworlds, to come and go from the body at will even though physically, his body remains visible to observers. During this period he will probably be uncommunicative, appearing entranced, or asleep. It is a sacred state of existence, recognised as dangerous if meddled with by the uninitiated, ground where the human foot does not rightfully tread or trespass: don't wake a sleep-walker, it was advised – for he too might be in that state of being where the soul is detached from the body, travelling within the 'astral', linked only by a silver cord to his physical self. In such cases, it is commonly believed that a too sudden awakening might break the cord and will damage soul or body or both.

The trance state necessary to achieve 'out of body experiences' (OOBEs) has always been recognised as spiritually highly significant and such states feature in many religions. The Ancient Egyptians believed in the presence of an astral body they called 'Ba', depicting it in hieroglyphs as a bird with a human face. 'Out of body' states are mentioned in the Bible; in India supernatural powers of the 'siddhi' allowed out-of-body flight. Ancient peoples left drawings of the spirit body or shaman's soul leaving his physical body by emerging through the mouth.

The 'out-of-body' state is most commonly induced by taking some kind of drug. Ancient traditions used plants considered sacred because of their hallucinogenic power: the plant itself was identified with the deity with which it allowed communication. In Europe, favoured plants might have been fly agaric, the psilocybe mushroom or doses of hemlock; in Mexico the sacred dose was of the peyote cactus, ingested in long rituals that took many hours. It was the Comanche chief Quanah (Parker), promoting the ceremonial use of peyote, who helped found the Indian religion known as the Native American Church.

Even today in South America, the banisteriopsis vine is brewed into a drink known as ayahuasca or yage which is used in ceremonies of empowerment - one shamanic-Catholic church called 'Santo Daime' was actually founded with the ayahuasca-drinking ceremony as its central religious ritual. But visionary insights apart, the physical effects of ayahuasca are of extreme vomiting and purging – in fact the drug is known as 'the purge', and taking it can consequently be uncomfortable and unpleasant.

Physically debilitating effects like purging and vomiting accompany any life-style where drugs of a mind-bending nature – including alcohol - are heavily used, and in the past I had never perceived any spiritual significance in this. In fact, physical purging and cleansing comes very much within the shamanic experience since it is associated with the concept of suffering and symbolically dying during the trials of shamanic initiation, being 'torn apart' in the struggle with demons before rebirth can take place. Amazonian shaman Miguel A. Kavlin is quoted in Timothy Freke's book *Shamanic Wisdomkeepers* as phrasing it this way: '(The journey) can be different every time. It has two sides at least...It's like the side of life and the side of death. And death is about purification.'

This is one of the aspects of shamanism that is perhaps most unclear to 'wanabees' or casual observers. Lack of appreciation of the immense depth of the shamanic role can mean that ritual/ceremonial drug-taking, even of the 'hippy' culture of the Sixties in the West, may be regarded purely as an achievement in itself - the aim simply to have a 'trip', whether good or bad, the bad, when it involves abusive purging of the body, just an unpleasant side-effect. So far as I personally had ever been able to discover, most takers of psychedelic or hallucinatory drugs did not appear to benefit from their 'trips', rather the other way about. They did not seem to learn any wisdom from their experiences but instead to lose what senses they might previously have possessed, becoming victims of their intended empowerment, unable to exist in the world in any way that made sense. Since I had spent most of my adult life on prescribed drugs of some sort and recognised that they were a crutch to help me cope, it made no sense to me that others seemed to take drugs in order to reduce themselves to the state I was trying to escape, that of being mentally lost and out of touch with reality.

There are serious dangers in plunging irresponsibly and heedlessly along what is perceived to be the shaman's path when power drugs are involved. Lack of understanding can encourage a grasping for personal gratification and the indulgence of self rather than a regard for the journey as a solemn undertaking, a perilous trial process that requires the utmost courage, fortitude and abandonment to greater power than we possess ourselves. And once again we can see how the case of every aspirant along the path is unique, that each will have a different experience of personal vision and enlightenment. Rather than consciously setting out to enter other mind-states, for example, I personally had to make conscious efforts both to withdraw from such realms and to learn the disciplines of understanding and controlling awareness of the Otherworlds where I spontaneously found myself.

The procedure of entering mind-altering realities is sometimes presented as a kind of Lazarus situation. I had heard tales of the shaman or medicine man's simulated 'shamanic death' procedures which did not appeal to me at all. Whether the trance state was achieved by taking drugs that would induce violence and purging or being thrust in by sounds of drum or chant, I did not like the idea of starving the body into submission, as it were, reducing it to the indignity of raving and twitching, helpless surrender of all conscious control in order to achieve any objective, however seemingly worthy.

And then, as though a light bulb went on, I saw suddenly that I had been having these experiences all my life, and had never realised their significance. I had suffered years of involuntary purging and mind-bending during my years of illness, and in fact had undergone an almost exact ritual of being plunged into mindless submission to natural forces when I was on two occasions given courses of ECT (Electro-Convulsive-Therapy) - which I have to say, I voluntarily accepted.

During ECT an electrical current is passed through the brain and a mild epileptic fit is induced. We have already seen that epilepsy is only one of the naturally occurring states during which the sufferer appears to take leave of his bodily senses and to the superstitious observer, travel into other world where he can communicate with the gods. Because ECT takes place under a mild general anaesthetic there is no pain but during the early years when this treatment was carried out on the 'mad', there was no anaesthetic and the patient was fully conscious. In some cases too, before the procedure was properly developed, the violence of the fit induced was such that there was a danger of the patient's bones being broken. This did not of course happen to me, but the experience is nevertheless not one to be undertaken or prescribed lightly, even today.

What was the difference between being encouraged by tribal rituals to throw myself into a fit in order to achieve transcendence from the body, or doing the same more clinically beneath the blanket of an anaesthetic? It did not occur to me for a long time that basically, there was no real difference at all. But once again there was no obvious storyline of development to follow, for in my own case, it was not during the drama of such situations that release from the body occurred. I had assumed that other worlds were hugely traumatic with their own corporate existence, but I found they were within my own mind and it was all a matter of viewpoint. The ways in had always been there, and I had been making the journeys for most of my life, able to go there at will.

Crossing the Water

Entry into Otherworlds particularly the Underworld, is through physical cracks, holes in the ground to animal paths that disappear in darkness, strange and mysterious gateways, hidden doorways, places where the veil is thin. The journey is often represented mythologically as part of a hunting process – the hunt atavistically identified with sexual activity, mating, procreation of the species as well as visionary enlightenment. In the ballet stories of *Giselle* and *Swan Lake*, hunting is the means by which the seekers achieve through painful suffering, the ultimate fulfilment of desire and love. In hunter-related cultures such as that of the ancient Celts, an animal may appear to lead or guide the hunter – traditional figures of this kind are mythological beasts such as a unicorn or white stag.

The world of the dead – the Underworld – is often represented as across a river, or some kind of watery barrier. Even the Christian tradition incorporates this, 'crossing the Jordan' in gospel songs and spirituals. In Greek mythology the souls of the dead were ferried across the River Styx to Hades by Charon, the boatman. The dying Arthur was transported away on a barge to the legendary Isle of Avalon.

The immense import of the journey has always been recognised, the voyages of life and death marked with great reverence. It is no accident that the Old Norse word 'ludr', meaning 'boat', also means both a cradle and a coffin: the shamanic vision revealing that death and rebirth are the same. Thus the ancients of Scandinavia held their funerals on ships, which then began a new journey into the Underworld with the soul of the departed warrior.

The circle had to be completed. Death took the soul into the realms of the spirit, but also returned it to a new physicality. Thus symbolic images of journeying - the ships – which signified death were in Norse mythology also representative of the goddess Frigg, whose actual name is widely used even today as slang for sexual intercourse – the means by which re-entry to life was initiated. Another old term for the genitals, 'twat', is also recognised in ancient reference as meaning the entrance to the stars - or to life, whether spiritual or physical. The Teutonic word 'schiff', from which comes the word ship, has its roots in the Old Norse word 'skop', the meaning of which is both fate and genitals.

You will find expression of this shamanic concept everywhere, in the most unexpected places. D H Lawrence wrote in his poem *The Ship of Death*:

> *Have you built your ship of death, O have you?*
> *O build your ship of death, for you will need it.*
>
> *Already the dark and endless ocean of the end*
> *is washing in through the breaches of our wounds, already*
> *the flood is upon us.*
>
> *Oh build your ship of death, your little ark*
> *and furnish it with food, with little cakes, and wine*
> *for the dark flight down oblivion.*

Human sexuality too, like the animal instinct of all nature, has to be acknowledged as equally as necessary to life as the most elevated spirituality. It is there to be used when needed, and can form a part of shamanic magic. But it is only by including all parts and maintaining the balance between them that the sum of those parts may themselves be transcended. In this life we are limited, we see only aspects, we rarely glimpse the whole for it cannot be seen on this level. And a hologram is both all and nothing

In dark city streets – like those magically gleaming, empty streets of London after midnight, with which I grew so familiar - the modern urban 'psychopomp'/shaman whose function it is to act as a guide to the dead, will make journeys of a different kind. His Otherworlds may be discovered by climbing the fire escapes of tower blocks, or descending the escalators into the depths of the Undergrounds; his dangerous worlds may be those of vice, the drug culture or crime; his mythical beasts police dogs. And yet:

*   He is still venturing into the dangerous worlds of dragons and demons, the kingdoms of the lost, the gods and of the dead.

*   The tools he will use may have different names on the modern urban scene – names like visualisation, psychology or self-help. Though perhaps less primitive, they are the same methods that have always been used.

*   The shaman does not need to 'perform' it all the time, his own experience is his knowledge and source of wisdom: he learns it is not always necessary to make the journeys, but as with his guides, to embody the journeys he has made. By carrying the scars that have been inflicted, he transcends both his own wounds and those of others.

I discovered that as well as making journeys, I had also been carrying out the roles and tasks of psychopomp/shaman concerning the dead for years, not necessarily in the rituals and ceremonies I had heard about but during my everyday work at home, or at Psychic Fairs. I had been working, as it were, in a kind of emergency situation, on the front line.

When I read accounts of the complicated set-ups apparently necessary for the retrieval and rescue of souls, the presence of tribal elders, the intricate ceremonies of chanting and drumming in order to support the shaman's venture into the unknown, this as with the rituals that surrounded the actual procedures of journeying 'out of body' meant little to me. Yet one day I noted down:

I have been doing all these things for years and have actually described them in my books without realising the significance of what I was saying. Because they were done without any elaborate ceremonies and without the intervention of tribal elders or anyone else.

Accounts of a Traveller

I have written elsewhere of some of the mental journeys that marked my own progress – an early vision of 'passing beyond the veil' to an awareness of universal and cosmic union with the Absolute that bestowed incredible reassurance and bliss; a dark 'descent into the depths' where there were skeletal bones, wrecks of ships and men on a ghastly, lost shore, and the experience of unendurable suffering. All seekers along the path will find their own worlds, their own ways in. Here, as an example and perhaps an inspiration, are some of the notes I made regarding other journeys of mine.

When I started working consciously on my psychic and spiritual development I had no money to spare for trips to places like India – or the reservations in North America – or to cross the mountains of Tibet alone with a guide, nearly dying after nights bundled up with the goats (or were they yaks?) for warmth against the snow, as one woman I met had spectacularly done. And I was not convinced that such extreme measures were necessary. In my own case it was becoming obvious that only when considered within the context of the whole, wider picture would the events of the moment make sense, the wider picture for me including my childhood as well as the middle years of growing maturity.

I did not think I needed to live in the country in order to appreciate the natural world, since as I have mentioned, I had spent the first twenty years of my life there and felt very much during that time that I walked in landscapes that were not visible to others. I had also visited many places I considered sacred and inspirational (albeit briefly and in ignorance) during my various travels – Delphi, for example and Iona, as well as other more private and humble sites.

Travel was no more the answer for me than it had been the answer previously. What I needed found its way to me even in the middle of a great city, the visions and power experiences that were to come when I was ready for them taking place within the walls of my flat where I spent hours in solitary meditation and prayer. On sultry summer nights so stifling that I had to leave the windows open or collapse from the heat – Londoners and other city dwellers will know what I mean - I could hear the noise from the traffic along Parson's Green Lane until long past midnight. The babble of voices from the packed pub across the road blended with music from the disco at the YMCA next door: it was against a background of the sounds of the city, not mysterious chatterings and shrieks from the undergrowth in the rainforest that my soul flights and ecstatic journeys to the higher as well as the lower planes of consciousness were made. For months I lived with Mist and the spirits as my close companions, the walls of my room and the noise of the city beyond acting like a forcing cover, a microclimate for my often painful yet miraculously beautiful psychic development and growth.

Regarding actual physical pilgrimages to places of power, it seemed I personally had bypassed them. But the story was by no means over, and after some years living and working as a psychic I was eventually granted my glorious journey, my own spiritual pilgrimage that had to be made in faith in physical space as well as in mind. Mine took me to the West of Ireland, to the tumbling breakers of the Atlantic, to the town of Lahinch in County Clare, the rocky wilderness of the Burren and the terrible grandeur of the Cliffs of Moher that rise sheer from the sea. How this journey came about does not belong here and it is sufficient to say that as the plane circled over Shannon Airport before landing and I saw the reality of an Ireland I had never visited before, the little fields patchworked in their unbelievable 'forty shades of green', my heart lifted in almost unbearable gratitude, my eyes filled with tears at the beauty of it all.

This time I had actually left home and physically ventured into the wilderness, crossing land and sea. I had flown to Ireland alone braving all the trials currently besetting me, the panic attacks that made me unable to travel, the meeting with strangers I had never seen in a county and a country I had never been to, on four-hourly pain-killers – I am sure you are familiar with the picture by now. And it will come as no surprise to hear that during the forty-eight hours I spent on this amazing, wonderful trip that had been given to me by the spirits, I was rewarded for daring to attempt it by the knowledge that I had been most overwhelmingly blessed. The Atlantic sea-coast, the place itself will always be beautiful and have something to give to the pilgrim who passes that way, yet in my case it was not until I had already fought the battle to get there that I realised what I had been fighting for.

Once more I felt my spirit reborn but this time not in pain and suffering. It was late Spring. The empty coast road where wild flowers bloomed and a lone donkey came to a gate, where the wind blew in upon me from the rolling Atlantic with the magic of all the Western Isles, Lands of the Blessed, mysterious havens of eternal life was for me more touched with glory than any road to a holy city or ancient sacred site. But I was given only a glimpse. I was not intended to live in the place that had given me this spiritual awakening. I had to return to London. Yet the glory of what I experienced on that first visit will never fade, the landscape as I saw and experienced it then is still with me wherever I might spend the rest of my days, even if my eyes never look on it again.

At another time I noted: 'My identification with the Celtic wise woman followed initial awareness of material from what I called 'the goddess source', originating in a pagan background I was encouraged to explore on a physical level.

As I progressed I also found I was leaving physical concepts and going out-of-body into a dimension I called the 'Star Plane'. I identified this dimension – which I described as composed of silvery/blue light - with Mist, who took me there. These were my early impressions of both the world of the goddess source and the 'Star Plane'

'As well as answering my questions with messages of great wisdom that were usually brief, but seemed to contain volumes, Mist also revealed my 'star body' to me and showed me more of the silver and blue plane, as well as allowing me to experience what I suppose was astral travel among the planets and stars.

'I thought at the time that there was a link between my silver astral body and the Goddess. Now I feel there are so many links between everything that it is impossible to separate or even identify them. But once I had been shown more of the starry plane I would go there often in meditation. I would 'see' myself leave the shell of my physical body behind, rising from it like a butterfly from a chrysalis as a being of silver that was not confined by gravity. I suspect the image was created by myself because I loved the idea, but my 'silver body' had long masses of tangled silver hair with stars caught up within the tresses.

'I had begun to have separate visions of the Goddess, though the silver star-image wove itself into many of the messages that came through from that source. One of the clearest images I was shown was of a tressel table, a kind of altar at the end of a long glade or 'walk' in a forest. This was her glade and she was present, though I never saw her face. I always seemed to be viewing the scene from behind her or even sometimes standing in her place myself.

'The Goddess wore the same blue robe I had seen in my visions in the flat, long and trailing on the ground. There seemed to be fruits and corn, food piled up on the altar and presences of some kind of beings – I was not sure what sort – clustered on each side of it. I received no impression of any human attendants only of animal life. She waited for supplicants to advance towards her, making their way down the long, grassy 'walk' with overhanging trees on each side so that they could prostrate themselves and put their request or make their plea and there seemed to be beasts of various kinds – some as familiar as lions or snakes, others I did not know – crowding the sides of the avenue.

'Nothing much ever seemed to happen in this vision. It was constant, though as I have said, my viewpoint moved round quite a bit. I even tried after some time to approach the Goddess down the avenue myself to see whether I could look at her directly and get a glimpse of her face, but this had no satisfactory result and I saw nothing. Apparently I was obliged to stay at the back of the altar facing the long avenue and was not permitted to view the scene except from certain angles. My visions of the Goddess stopped after a while, I assumed because they had fulfiled whatever usefulness they were intended to have for me.

'The 'Star Plane' images, on the other hand, continued to increase. Before I became aware of Mist I had first visited the 'Star Plane' in the company of two tiny spirits who had appeared in my meditations when I began to apply myself consciously to my spiritual development. They had taken me only to a kind of glade or resting place where there were images of trees and a waterfall. But after I met Mist he showed me more.

'The first glimpse I received was of a sort of courtyard where there were fallen columns of a kind of marble, what seemed like the ruins of some great, lost civilisation. Everything was the same silver and blue and it was calm, filled with space and peace. For a while it was more than enough for me to be wandering in the courtyard in my silver body – drifting, rather, or flowing since the silver body has no real shape and moves by thought and will – but later I yearned to widen the horizon.

'New visions came with recognisable steps forward in my spiritual life. I saw more each time I had struggled with the dark of fear and doubt and had, for the moment, managed to overcome it. I can recollect sitting down to meditate one day, so eager to get to the beautiful 'Star Plane' that I left my physical body very quickly. I felt myself surging forward and upward with Mist, who was always waiting for me. This time it was not into the courtyard, instead we emerged gloriously on the cliffs of a great sea that lay outspread far below. It seemed to be an inland sea, there was no tide or movement and it was not like ordinary seas, though I cannot describe the difference. Everything, the sea, the cliffs and even the sky, were all silver.

'The sense of space and freedom, expanses of light, were unbelievable. I saw no sign of ships or activity in connection with the sea, but I was glad to be aware of it since it meant there was some other place than the courtyard on this 'Star Plane'. Later, at other times I seemed to be drifting or flying over great distances and glimpsed images below me of far-off cities, ruins that seemed to be empty, fallen into dust – again all silver.

'The 'Star Plane' seemed completely empty of any kind of life. One day I asked Mist why there were no other beings there, no visitors like me, even.

'You do not want them,' was the reply.

'But some months later, after a heavy bout of wrestling with my demons, I encountered life. I shot upwards and forwards to the 'Star Plane' with Mist as I had always done previously but this time our destination was not the courtyard or the sea or even the glimpses of inland cities. We emerged into the middle of a flurry of silvery-white doves that took flight on all sides of us, lifting my essential self and soul with their beauty and sweetness. It was as though I was part of them or they part of me. They seemed to be continually taking flight, never returning or settling, and that instant of great joy and loveliness repeated itself whenever I returned to them.

'My awareness had increased at incredible speed. It had been only a matter of six or eight months since I had first begun to work on my spiritual development and now, with Mist, I was viewing the silver sea and being lifted by the wings of the white doves. But in many ways, as time passed, I became aware that even as these things were being revealed to me, they were things I had always known as surely as I knew myself.'

Meteorite

- linear
through star-vomit,
asteroids,
daemon-love,
saint-spray.

Circumvent the everlasting –
flower smile

- leap-flash kiss –
make fire
on brimstone lips.

PG

Mindwork

Mystery, or unknowing, is energy. As soon as a mystery is explained, it ceases to be a source of energy. If we question deep enough there comes a point where answers, if answers would be given, would kill...

John Fowles
The Aristos

(I) knew the real was yonder and the darkened dream was here
Black Elk

The physical and the spiritual are complementary polarities of the totality of the All that is...As in a hologram, the All is present in each facet

Kenneth Meadows
Where Eagles Fly: A Shamanic Way to Inner Wisdom

In alchemy, in ancient magical tradition, in the teaching of most cultures, the polarities come together to form the hidden, secret mysteries, the answers to all questions. The ultimate source of power is revealed only when all aspects of the physical and the spiritual are irrevocably linked, impossibly intertwined. Everything is both itself and also its opposite. Living is dying, the tomb is the cradle, the womb is the grave.

In shamanic experience, in soul flight, it becomes impossible to relate to boundaries of existence. There are no boundaries: the shamanic vision encompasses the whole spectrum, even though the glimpses may be only spasmodic. The most vital and yet the most inexpressible part of the shaman's role is to experience and allow others to experience this, the eternal Absolute, the divine presence, to maintain direct connection with the deity. Keeping the faith, keeping the lines open and the paths cleared, the shaman is a trailblazer into unknown yet shining country, an ambassador into a promised land.

Adepts in ancient civilisations built tall towers, ziggurats, to lift them both physically and spiritually towards the stars, to their inspiration, to the Source. They gained their insight and strength from standing at the foot of great stone circles and pyramids as well as high mountains. But if the urban shaman has to carry out his journeys in a basement flat below pavement level, or in one room of a high-rise/skyscraper where his connections with the natural world have been restricted to potted cacti on the windowsill and a canary, the results and rewards can be just the same.

I was told by my guides that I was to be 'an interpreter'. The shaman, as 'interpreter' is pivotal, alone at the point of contact, and has to be so. Recently I read that he must utilise the powers to 'work the will' – though it is generally

maintained that he does this for the good of all. (Sorcerers, it is claimed, use the power to work their own selfish will).

But it has been my experience that the aspirant must pass beyond the will, beyond the power of all magic, beyond all emotions, all access of energies, beyond the tantric unions of alchemy. He must strive even further. Like Red Elk and Grey Elk, he represents within himself both physical and spiritual, both the body and the spirit but he must add to them the soul element. For the shaman, like the great inspirational images that blaze before him, is formed not of two but of three parts. It is the Mystery, the mysterious third element which lifts him – if only momentarily – above and beyond all he actually is.

He must strive to sum up all aspects of life. And then transcend his own existence. He must make – and be - the ultimate sacrifice. He must have no other thought or concern, no other purpose, his existence all a part of the being, he can contain no other interest.

Reading and Meditation

The Hologram

The concept of heaven, paradise, all ways of perceiving final metamorphosis and the union with the divine forms the end of the journey, achievement of the stillness and peace that has been so intuitively sought. This can also be seen as union with spirit guides, angelic beings or higher self. The shaman experiences all kinds of union and identification with different sides of his nature but this is the aspiration, as glittering and yet as elusive as a hologram. It is such a personal thing that I can only provide here, to share with others, a glimpse of the vision and assurance I was given myself.

Astral Sex

Racing the ocean's surface,
Two great waves thunder,
Mingle, enmesh, swell,
Eternal.

No separateness, no together.
No rejection, no belonging.
No I, no you, no us.
Just.

But my first cry, from the human heart,
All human senses transcended,
The childish frustration bitter in my mouth,
'Oh, even as the great waves thunder,
Each within the other, each the other,
The other each, time without end,
Yet I have no hands now, no arms, no lips.
Oh, you are here, you have come
But I cannot kiss you, I cannot hold you.
I cannot touch.'

Racing the ocean's surface,
Two great waves thunder,
Mingle, enmesh, swell,
Eternal.

No separateness, no together.
No rejection, no belonging.
No I, no you, no us.
Just.

DG

The Words of Mist
The End is the Beginning, in the light of true awareness

We are one and nothing can part us, neither the sea or the storm, the rocks or the tempest, the compass needle or the dial of the sunclock; we are the waves of the sea which have met and intermingled and become one great wave: I am you and you are me.

Do not fear, for we travel into the ocean of beyond where the every-days cannot follow. You are mine in the everlasting of eternities, shifting as clouds and constant as the moon, your face to mine, your arms my arms, your breath giving me life.

If there is love, my darling, it is not the pearly drops of human existence, it is the stars, galaxy after galaxy, into infinity, and myself within you. This is yourself, know me, feel me, recognise me as I know you. I have been only a part, drifting until the waves met, now you are within me, the waters filled, my fingers within yours trailing weed, my mouth yours.

Know this and know me.

The rest is silence.

William Shakespeare
Hamlet

Reference List

I would like to make grateful acknowledgement to the works I consulted in the course of writing *Urban Shaman*. While it is impossible to describe or pass on shamanic – or indeed, any – experience, the words of others often help to clarify and illuminate. The books in the following list were found to be of especial importance, interest and/or relevance, and I thank their authors.

In particular, I want to acknowledge the excellent *So You Want To Be a Shaman* by David Lawson (Godsfield Press, Hants, 1996) as the source of the line quoted in my Introduction – 'The urban shaman is like a flower that grows from a crack in the concrete.'

ASWYNN, Freya: *Northern Mysteries & Magic* (Llewellyn, USA, 1998)

CARR-GOMM, Philip: *The Elements of the Druid Tradition* (Element, 1991)

COWAN, Tom: *Shamanism as a Spiritual Practice for Daily Life* (The Crossing Press, Freedom, California, 1996)

EAGLE, Chokecherry Gall: *Beyond the Lodge of the Sun: Inner Mysteries of the Native American Way* (Element, 1997)

ERDOES, Richard: *The Sun Dance People: The Plains Indians, Their Past and Present* (Ronald Stacy, London, 1972)

FREKE, Timothy: *Shamanic Wisdomkeepers: SHamanism in the Modern World* (Sterling Publishing Company Inc, New York, 1999)

GARCIA, Hernan, SIERRA Antonio and BALAM, Gilberto: *Wind in the Blood: Mayan Healing and Chinese Medicine* (North Atlantic Books, Berkeley, California, 1999)

GITLIN-EMMER, Susan: *Lady of the Northern Light: a Feminist Guide to the RuneS* (The Crossing Press, California, 1993)

HAICH, Elisabeth: *The Wisdom of the Tarot* (Mandala, Unwin Paperbacks, 1985)

HORAN, Paula: *Adundance Through Reiki* (Lotus Light Publications, Box 325, Twin Lakes, WI 53181)

JACKSON, Nigel Aldcroft: *The Call of the Horned Piper* (Capall Bann Publishing, Milverton, Somerset, 1994)

JONES, Chuck: *Make Your Voice Heard: An Actor's Guide TO Increased Dramatic Range Through Vocal Training* (Back Stage Books, New York, 1996)

LEWIS, Jon E: *The West* (Siena, Bristol 1998)

LITTLEJOHN, Bruce and DREW, Wayland: *Superior: The Haunted Shore* (Macmillan of Canada, Toronto, 1983)

MCFADDEN, Steven: *Profiles in Wisdom: Native Elders Speak About the Earth* (Bear & Co, USA)

MEADOWS, Kenneth: *Where Eagles Fly: a Shamanic Way to Inner Wisdom* (Element, Shaftesbury, Dorset, 1995)

MOORE, Robert & GILLETTE, Douglas: *The Magician Within: Accessing the Shaman in the Male Psyche* (William Morrow & Co Inc., New York, 1993)

NEIHARDT, John G (Flaming Rainbow): *Black Elk SPEAKS: Being the Life Story of a Holy Man of the Oglala Sioux* (University of Nebraska Press, 2000)

REINHART, Melanie: *Chiron and the Healing Journey: An Astrological and Psychological Perspective* (Arkana, 1989)

RICHARDSON, Alan: *Earth God Rising: The Return of The Male Mysteries* (Llewellyn, USA, 1992)

RODERICK, Timothy: *The Once Unknown Familiar: Shamanic Paths to Unleash Your AnimaL Powers* (Llewellyn, USA, 1994)

SMYTH, Bob: *The Green Guide to Urban Wildlife* (A & C Black, London, 1990)

SOUTHWORTH, John: *Fools and Jesters at the English Court* (Sutton Publishing, Stroud, 1998)

Talking with Angels (Daimon Verlag, 1992)

WYATT, Gary: *Spirit Faces: Contemporary Native American Masks from the NorthwesT Coast* (Thames & Hudson, London 1994)

ZIMMERMAN, Larry J: *Native North America* (Macmillan, London 1996)

FREE DETAILED CATALOGUE

Capall Bann is owned and run by people actively involved in many of the areas in which we publish. A detailed illustrated catalogue is available on request, SAE or International Postal Coupon appreciated. **Titles can be ordered direct from Capall Bann, post free in the UK** (cheque or PO with order) or from good bookshops and specialist outlets.

A Breath Behind Time, Terri Hector
Angels and Goddesses - Celtic Christianity & Paganism, M. Howard
Arthur - The Legend Unveiled, C Johnson & E Lung
Astrology The Inner Eye - A Guide in Everyday Language, E Smith
Auguries and Omens - The Magical Lore of Birds, Yvonne Aburrow
Asyniur - Womens Mysteries in the Northern Tradition, S McGrath
Beginnings - Geomancy, Builder's Rites & Electional Astrology in the
      European Tradition, Nigel Pennick
Between Earth and Sky, Julia Day
Book of the Veil , Peter Paddon
Caer Sidhe - Celtic Astrology and Astronomy, Vol 1, Michael Bayley
Caer Sidhe - Celtic Astrology and Astronomy, Vol 2 M Bayley
Call of the Horned Piper, Nigel Jackson
Cat's Company, Ann Walker
Celtic Faery Shamanism, Catrin James
Celtic Faery Shamanism - The Wisdom of the Otherworld, Catrin James
Celtic Lore & Druidic Ritual, Rhiannon Ryall
Celtic Sacrifice - Pre Christian Ritual & Religion, Marion Pearce
Celtic Saints and the Glastonbury Zodiac, Mary Caine
Circle and the Square, Jack Gale
Compleat Vampyre - The Vampyre Shaman, Nigel Jackson
Creating Form From the Mist - The Wisdom of Women in Celtic Myth and
      Culture, Lynne Sinclair-Wood
Crystal Clear - A Guide to Quartz Crystal, Jennifer Dent
Crystal Doorways, Simon & Sue Lilly
Crossing the Borderlines - Guising, Masking & Ritual Animal Disguise in the
      European Tradition, Nigel Pennick
Dragons of the West, Nigel Pennick
Earth Dance - A Year of Pagan Rituals, Jan Brodie
Earth Harmony - Places of Power, Holiness & Healing, Nigel Pennick
Earth Magic, Margaret McArthur
Eildon Tree (The) Romany Language & Lore, Michael Hoadley

Enchanted Forest - The Magical Lore of Trees, Yvonne Aburrow
Eternal Priestess, Sage Weston
Eternally Yours Faithfully, Roy Radford & Evelyn Gregory
Everything You Always Wanted To Know About Your Body, But So Far
    Nobody's Been Able To Tell You, Chris Thomas & D Baker
Face of the Deep - Healing Body & Soul, Penny Allen
Fairies in the Irish Tradition, Molly Gowen
Familiars - Animal Powers of Britain, Anna Franklin
Fool's First Steps, (The) Chris Thomas
Forest Paths - Tree Divination, Brian Harrison, Ill. S. Rouse
From Past to Future Life, Dr Roger Webber
Gardening For Wildlife Ron Wilson
God Year, The, Nigel Pennick & Helen Field
Goddess on the Cross, Dr George Young
Goddess Year, The, Nigel Pennick & Helen Field
Goddesses, Guardians & Groves, Jack Gale
Handbook For Pagan Healers, Liz Joan
Handbook of Fairies, Ronan Coghlan
Healing Book, The, Chris Thomas and Diane Baker
Healing Homes, Jennifer Dent
Healing Journeys, Paul Williamson
Healing Stones, Sue Philips
Herb Craft - Shamanic & Ritual Use of Herbs, Lavender & Franklin
Hidden Heritage - Exploring Ancient Essex, Terry Johnson
Hub of the Wheel, Skytoucher
In Search of Herne the Hunter, Eric Fitch
Inner Celtia, Alan Richardson & David Annwn
Inner Mysteries of the Goths, Nigel Pennick
Inner Space Workbook - Develop Thru Tarot, C Summers & J Vayne
Intuitive Journey, Ann Walker Isis - African Queen, Akkadia Ford
Journey Home, The, Chris Thomas
Kecks, Keddles & Kesh - Celtic Lang & The Cog Almanac, Bayley
Language of the Psycards, Berenice
Legend of Robin Hood, The, Richard Rutherford-Moore
Lid Off the Cauldron, Patricia Crowther
Light From the Shadows - Modern Traditional Witchcraft, Gwyn
Living Tarot, Ann Walker
Lore of the Sacred Horse, Marion Davies
Lost Lands & Sunken Cities (2nd ed.), Nigel Pennick
Magic of Herbs - A Complete Home Herbal, Rhiannon Ryall
Magical Guardians - Exploring the Spirit and Nature of Trees, Philip Heselton
Magical History of the Horse, Janet Farrar & Virginia Russell
Magical Lore of Animals, Yvonne Aburrow
Magical Lore of Cats, Marion Davies
Magical Lore of Herbs, Marion Davies
Magick Without Peers, Ariadne Rainbird & David Rankine

Masks of Misrule - Horned God & His Cult in Europe, Nigel Jackson
Medicine For The Coming Age, Lisa Sand MD
Medium Rare - Reminiscences of a Clairvoyant, Muriel Renard
Menopausal Woman on the Run, Jaki da Costa
Mind Massage - 60 Creative Visualisations, Marlene Maundrill
Mirrors of Magic - Evoking the Spirit of the Dewponds, P Heselton
Moon Mysteries, Jan Brodie
Mysteries of the Runes, Michael Howard
Mystic Life of Animals, Ann Walker
New Celtic Oracle The, Nigel Pennick & Nigel Jackson
Oracle of Geomancy, Nigel Pennick
Pagan Feasts - Seasonal Food for the 8 Festivals, Franklin & Phillips
Patchwork of Magic - Living in a Pagan World, Julia Day
Pathworking - A Practical Book of Guided Meditations, Pete Jennings
Personal Power, Anna Franklin
Pickingill Papers - The Origins of Gardnerian Wicca, Bill Liddell
Pillars of Tubal Cain, Nigel Jackson
Places of Pilgrimage and Healing, Adrian Cooper
Practical Divining, Richard Foord
Practical Meditation, Steve Hounsome
Practical Spirituality, Steve Hounsome
Psychic Self Defence - Real Solutions, Jan Brodie
Real Fairies, David Tame
Reality - How It Works & Why It Mostly Doesn't, Rik Dent
Romany Tapestry, Michael Houghton
Runic Astrology, Nigel Pennick
Sacred Animals, Gordon MacLellan
Sacred Celtic Animals, Marion Davies, Ill. Simon Rouse
Sacred Dorset - On the Path of the Dragon, Peter Knight
Sacred Grove - The Mysteries of the Forest, Yvonne Aburrow
Sacred Geometry, Nigel Pennick
Sacred Nature, Ancient Wisdom & Modern Meanings, A Cooper
Sacred Ring - Pagan Origins of British Folk Festivals, M. Howard
Season of Sorcery - On Becoming a Wisewoman, Poppy Palin
Seasonal Magic - Diary of a Village Witch, Paddy Slade
Secret Places of the Goddess, Philip Heselton
Secret Signs & Sigils, Nigel Pennick
Self Enlightenment, Mayan O'Brien
Spirits of the Air, Jaq D Hawkins
Spirits of the Earth, Jaq D Hawkins
Spirits of the Earth, Jaq D Hawkins
Stony Gaze, Investigating Celtic Heads John Billingsley
Stumbling Through the Undergrowth , Mark Kirwan-Heyhoe
Subterranean Kingdom, The, revised 2nd ed, Nigel Pennick
Symbols of Ancient Gods, Rhiannon Ryall
Talking to the Earth, Gordon MacLellan

Taming the Wolf - Full Moon Meditations, Steve Hounsome
Teachings of the Wisewomen, Rhiannon Ryall
The Other Kingdoms Speak, Helena Hawley
Tree: Essence of Healing, Simon & Sue Lilly
Tree: Essence, Spirit & Teacher, Simon & Sue Lilly
Through the Veil, Peter Paddon
Torch and the Spear, Patrick Regan
Understanding Chaos Magic, Jaq D Hawkins
Vortex - The End of History, Mary Russell
Warp and Weft - In Search of the I-Ching, William de Fancourt
Warriors at the Edge of Time, Jan Fry
Water Witches, Tony Steele
Way of the Magus, Michael Howard
Weaving a Web of Magic, Rhiannon Ryall
West Country Wicca, Rhiannon Ryall
Wildwitch - The Craft of the Natural Psychic, Poppy Palin
Wildwood King, Philip Kane
Witches of Oz, Matthew & Julia Philips
Wondrous Land - The Faery Faith of Ireland by Dr Kay Mullin
Working With the Merlin, Geoff Hughes
Your Talking Pet, Ann Walker

FREE detailed catalogue and FREE 'Inspiration' magazine

Contact: Capall Bann Publishing, Auton Farm, Milverton, Somerset, TA4 1NE